To Wilma Carpenter

# DOC

## THE LIFE OF
## EMILY HAMMOND WILSON

Emily H. Wilson

For Aunt Willie with love
and admiration from
your niece, the Author,

T. Magnotti

BY
THERESE MAGNOTTI

Published by the
Shady Side Rural Heritage Society, Inc.,
P.O. Box 89
Shady Side, MD 20764
410.867.4486.

Printed by Whitmore Print & Imaging, Annapolis, MD

ISBN 0-9653536-0-5

# ACKNOWLEDGEMENTS

I've read that, for the sake of impartiality, a biographer should not become enamored of the subject. In the case of Emily Wilson, this restriction is impossible. I confess to becoming beguiled by the forthcoming manner in which she described the recollections of a lifetime, spoken in her softly accented voice with utmost candor and with a wonderful sense of the outrageous.

To Emily Wilson I extend my most devoted thanks.

Thank you to John, Chris and Bettie Wilson, to Jon Frisby and to Julian and Nikki Hammond for insight, information and hospitality.

Thank you to Glorious Shenton, Sally Whall, Mattie Moreland, Margie Moreland, Marjorie Kolb and Harry Ford for filling in some gaps.

Thank you to my husband, John, who provided both encouragement and valuable criticism, and who taught me to use the computer, sort of.

Thank you to Mavis Daly for allowing me to lean upon her so heavily and to the Board of the Shady Side Rural Heritage Society, Inc., for its patience, interest and support.

Thank you to George Shenk for his advice and for walking me through the printing process.

Finally, thank you to my friend, Barbara Owings, who volunteered me for this project one day when I was absent.

Therese Magnotti
Shady Side, Maryland, 1996

For John

*I look back on it now and wonder how I had the energy to do the things I did. Somehow it didn't seem too difficult in those days. You just took things as they came along...you got to the stream and you went across it.*

*...some very nice things happened*

*Emily Hammond Wilson, M.D.*

Baltimore, Maryland, 1929.

It was a beautiful Saturday morning. The warm breeze from the harbor filtered around the buildings and into the city, luffing the patriotic bunting festooned on the street lamps. The sun was beginning to warm the bricks even at such an early hour, and the brilliant blue of the sky promised a good weekend for Decoration Day festivities. As she looked from her window to check the day, the young woman saw only a few people on the streets. "Everybody must be sleeping in today," she thought, as she glanced at her two roommates cocooned on their cots. Dressing quickly, she drank her coffee standing up, smoking in nervous puffs at the window, watching a train spewing soot and smoke as it left Mt. Royal Station. She put out her cigarette, placed her empty cup in the sink, and gathering up her purse and papers, she slipped quietly out of the apartment and down the stairs to the street.

As she hurried along to the bus station, she took time to recheck her appearance in a shop window. Reflected in the glass, she saw a short and slender young woman with a dark cap of hair, dressed in a summery frock. Her shoes were "sensible." She was, after all, going down to the country where high-heeled pumps sank into the grass the length of their shank. "If I don't look right, there's nothing I can do about it now," she shrugged.

There were several people waiting for the bus, and the young woman joined them on the corner, waiting in shy silence. Shortly, the old bus came wheezing up to the stop, the passengers climbed up the steps, gave the driver their tickets, and selected their seats. With a slam of the door and grinding of gears, the bus lurched from the station, beginning its trip through the city of Baltimore and down Route 2 into the southern Maryland countryside.

The young woman sat alone gazing through the grimy window as the bus chugged and clattered along the corkscrew-turned road. She didn't notice the vistas changing from city to country or that the bus stopped to

1

let passengers off or on. Deep in her own thoughts, she wondered how she would be received by Mr. Hutchins, the man she was to meet in Friendship. Her usual jaunty confidence seemed to have deserted her. Striking off alone, she was taking her first trip to the southern part of the county where she knew no one, and wasn't sure exactly where she was going to sleep that night. There were no busses back to Baltimore until the next day.

At about two in the afternoon, the bus halted at the general store in the crossroads village of Friendship. The young woman stepped down from the bus along with a young man, her fellow bus passenger. He held the door for her, and together they entered the store, passing from bright sunlight into semi-shade. As her eyes adjusted, the young woman saw a typical general store, offering some foodstuffs, some clothing, and some of nearly everything. She noticed an ice cream dipper in a dish of water and a round cheese on the counter, but her survey of the interior stopped when her eyes came to rest on an older man standing near the cash drawer. The man questioned her traveling companion:

"You know, Rob, there was a young doctor who was supposed to come down on that bus from Baltimore today. Did you see him get off the bus?"

"Nossir, Mr. Hutchins. Nobody got off the bus with me but this lady, here."

"Well, I wonder what could have happened to him?" he mused.

With trembling knees and extending the letter of introduction in her shaking hand, the young woman approached Mr. Hutchins, and spoke.

"I am Emily Cumming Hammond, and I am the doctor you are expecting."

# ONE

I was born at Redcliffe, South Carolina, at 4:00 o'clock on the hot Friday afternoon of July 8th, 1904. I was the first child of Mary Gwynn Hammond and Christopher Cashiel Fitzsimons Hammond. My birth had been expected all day, and family legend says that Hester, the family cook, became so excited when my arrival was announced, that she threw a ham she had been preparing for dinner out the window!

The plantation, Redcliffe, came to my great-grandfather, James Henry Hammond, through his marriage to a 16-year old heiress, Catherine Fitzsimons. Redcliffe was built in 1859, and is named for the red bluffs on the riverbank in front of the house. My great-grandfather was a believer in states' rights and quite a notorious man. He was governor of South Carolina (the family refers to him as "the Governor")*. It was he, as a United States Senator, who pronounced on the Senate floor, "Cotton is King!" and who made the secession speech when South Carolina seceeded from the Union. Upon the election of Abraham Lincoln, he declined into discouragement and died embittered before the end of the Civil War. By that time, he had enlarged his holdings to 14,000 acres.

At the time of my birth, Redcliffe was the plantation home of my paternal grandparents, Emily Cumming Hammond, for whom I was named, and Major James Henry Hammond (Harry). My grandfather had fought during the War Between the States on General Gregg's staff. When he returned from the War, he found a trunk full of worthless Confederate bills in the attic and a vastly changed society.

Grandfather Hammond studied medicine at the University of Pennsylvania, at the College of Charleston, and in Heidelberg, Germany, but didn't believe in sending his own children to school! Instead my father and his two brothers were sent to the neighbor's house to be taught the primary grades. At least once a month my grandmother would look out the window to see the three little boys trudging back up the hill to Redcliffe, dragging their small chairs, having been expelled for some disciplinary infraction. Redcliffe's library was full of books, and my grandfather was of the opinion that everybody in the family would wake up one morning and be able to read ... because **all** the family read.

My earliest memory of my grandmother Hammond is that she sat in a rocking chair in the library, wearing a white lace cap. Her rocking chair had been made of canvas by her son, my Uncle Henry. It swung on a

---

*Bleser, Carol; "The Hammonds of Redcliffe"; Oxford Univ. Press, 1981 ISBN 0-10-502920-8. "Secret and Sacred. Diaries of James Henry Hammond, a Southern Shareholder," edited by Carol Bleser, Oxford Univ. Press, 1988 ISBN 0-19-505308-7.

pivot, and Uncle Henry said it was the nearest thing to his mother's lap he could think of. Uncle Henry had one of the first Victrolas sent to Redcliffe because grandmother loved music. All the other Hammonds had tin ears.

My mother's grandfather, Andrew Jackson Gwynn, was a captain during the War Between the States, and was badly injured by a bayonet at Sharpsburg. After the War, he and his wife, Mary Louise Keene, left their native Prince George's County, Maryland, and migrated to Spartanburg, South Carolina, where he entered the textile business. The Gwynns were devout Catholics, and, since they were the first Catholic family in that part of South Carolina, they began a little Catholic church in Spartanburg. Later their son, my uncle Andrew Keene Gwynn, became a priest and a missionary in the northern part of South Carolina.

Julia Hammond, my father's sister, was born before the Civil War. As a young woman she had enrolled at Radcliffe College, but left after three months because she was homesick. She married James Richards when she was in her fifties, and they never had children.

One of my earliest memories is of Aunt Julia riding her horse from Redcliffe down to our home at Kathwood for dinner. From the time I was about three or four, well before I started school, she frequently invited me to return with her for a day or two. I sat on a cushion in front of her saddle and rode with her on her horse up to Redcliffe. Aunt Julia particularly liked storms. She always chose to start back in a thunderstorm, if one were about, and I remember shivering with nervous excitement at the prospect.

Later when we children were a little older, Aunt Julia would have house parties for all of her nieces and nephews, sometimes lasting for two weeks at a time. How she could tolerate us, I don't know; but we had wonderful times. We'd have melons and fruits for breakfast, followed by eggs and bacon and anything one might wish. We rode horseback to one of the two ponds on the farm to go swimming. Each of us claimed a room on the third floor at Redcliffe, and we pretended our room was "our house."

We dressed up in all the old clothes that had been left there, went down to the parlor, put a record on grandmother's Victrola and danced the minuet or the waltz. We didn't wear our own clothes for the entire two weeks, but wore either a bathing suit or fancy dress. We ruined all these beautiful old clothes, but when my cousin, John Billings, bought the house in 1935, he'd have thrown them all out anyway.

# TWO

*You know, things didn't seem to have changed much from the way people lived in the Governor's time to the way we lived in the early days at Kathwood.*

*Emily H. Wilson*

About six months after I was born, my parents moved to Kathwood. Originally called "Cedar Grove," Kathwood had been renamed by the Governor in honor of his wife. It was a typical house of the time, with a central hall and a staircase, with four large rooms on each floor. Later we added what we called the "annex." It contained a kitchen, a pantry and porch, and a bathroom was added onto the back. In the earliest days there were few amenities, but we did have a bathroom as far back as I can remember. Having only the one bathroom for all of us was sometimes a hassle. There was no central heat, but each room had a fireplace. The place could get as cold as a barn on winter mornings, and very often my father would get up and light all the fires himself first thing. He warned us not to stand on the hearth "unless it snowed." You know how often it snows in South Carolina.

It was at Kathwood that my brothers and sisters were born. We were a large family: Harry, Julian, Keene, Louise, Chris, Katharine, Mary and myself, and a first cousin, the child of my mother's brother. We called him J.B. His father had died before he was born, and he had proven to be a disciplinary problem for his mother in Spartanburg. Mother took him to Kathwood ... as though she didn't have enough to do with the eight of us. He came when he was in second grade and stayed with us through high school, so we were nine children in all. My youngest brother, Julian, was the last child born to my parents, and there are fifteen years between our ages. Although we were born quite closely together, there were four older children, and then four younger ones. Each of the older children had to adopt one of the younger ones to care for. The oldest of the second crowd was my brother Christopher; but one of my sisters decided she wanted him, so I took care of Keene. We were four girls and four boys, and so there were two double beds in each of two bedrooms. My parents had one bedroom, and our teacher, Miss Wilson and our nurse, Shooney, shared the fourth bedroom.

In spite of having no money, we had a very happy childhood on the whole, with wonderful amounts of security, affection and devotion from not only our parents, but from Shooney and Hester, our cook. We had a great deal of freedom to enjoy all the activities of the country, such as having a horse to ride and being able to swim in the mill pond ... some of the country entertainments that most people have forgotten these days.

As I look back on it now, it is difficult for me to describe my wonder at our father's various enterprises undertaken to keep his large household together. Primarily he was a planter, but he was extremely clever at finding positions which would augment his farming at Kathwood. My father experimented with growing different crops in an attempt to avoid some of the gamble he took with cotton. He had 1500 acres in prime cotton, but those years when the bottom fell out of the cotton market, the crop might fetch only ten cents per pound. There was no control over the price of cotton, but farmers planted it hoping it would bring enough money to at least last the year. However, the cotton factors in Augusta would control the prices, so one never knew what to expect. Of course, when cotton was baled, it could be held indefinitely; but the farmer had to pay for storage while he waited for the price to improve. Sometimes the price didn't go up, so he was caught in a dilemma.

He tried planting tobacco at one time, and also tried growing rice, but there was no machinery for threshing the rice, so it didn't really work out. Then we tried a crop of tomatoes. We shipped one carload, which sold for a small profit in New York, but the second carload did not sell. Eventually, we got enough from the insurance to pay the shipping charges to New York, and that was all the income we got from the second tomato crop. The great trouble with all of this produce was being able to find a market for it. We were competing with people who lived on the coast, who got their tomatoes planted earlier, and who had regular customers to whom to sell their crops. There was no refrigeration in those days, so they picked the tomatoes very green and wrapped them separately by hand, put them into crates and loaded them on freight cars. If they weren't sold within a few days, they rotted.

Daddy ran the grist mill built by my great-grandfather on a creek running through the land. The mill provided meal and flour not only for Kathwood, but for other farmers in the neighborhood. They paid Daddy a certain portion of the meal he ground for them. Later he did go into it more commercially because there came to be a market for water-ground meal and grits. Water power, it was said, ground the corn slowly, giving the meal a better taste than corn ground by machine. There was a cotton gin in the same location, all powered by the same pond. Near the mill, was a large storage building called "the seed house," where the cotton seed was stored. He bought the cotton seed for the Southern Cotton Oil Company on commission, and that was one of his few cash incomes. There was very little cash money from anything.

In connection with the mill, Daddy had a small country store, and the man who ran the store doubled as Daddy's bookkeeper. You could buy salt pork or fatback, and there was always a big round cheese, packages of crackers, chewing tobacco for the workers, and soft drinks; and we thought it perfectly wonderful if we could wangle a nickle, but Daddy made us pay for the soft drinks. There were Nabisco crackers in tin boxes for ten cents, and if you earned ten cents, it was the height of luxury! It was a very busy place, and we were not allowed to walk around in bathing suits, even though the bathing suits came down to our knees and we wore black stockings. Daddy felt it was a bad example for the people working around the mill.

He was appointed Justice of the Peace and was licensed to perform marriages, and he sometimes had to intercede in fights and domestic arguments on the farm. Finally, Daddy was the freight agent at Kathwood Station for the railroad, which allowed us a certain amount of free transportation and other benefits, especially a cash income. His salary was $15 per month. The conductors, his buddies on the railroad, sometimes brought a barrel of oysters up from the coast in the wintertime, and he met the train at the station. When the train slowed down, the package was thrown off the train. The seafood varied our menus quite a bit. How Daddy ever survived with so many of us to care for and so many uncertainties, I don't know!

The little school in Beech Island had been built on land donated by my grandfather. It was known as the Downer School, because Mr. Downer had donated the money to construct the building. The school spanned first-grade through what passed as high school in those days. Mother was a schoolteacher, and after teaching kindergarden in Charleston, she had been accepted by my grandfather to teach first and second grades in Beech Island. My mother and father met there in Beech Island. He fell head over heels and never stopped loving her.

Mother boarded with a very kind family in the neighborhood, and they furnished her with a horse and buggy to go to Mass in Augusta every Sunday. My father joined the Catholic Church before he and Mother were married. The story goes that my grandmother Hammond had to hear his catechism - and he was 32 years old at the time!

My mother was a pioneer. She was the first Catholic in the Beech Island area, and that was difficult at times. She initiated the literary society for the people in the neighborhood and even supported womens' suffrage. So many people who grew up in the country never had a chance at education, but Mother, having been a teacher, told us, "We will probably never have money enough to leave you anything when we die, but we hope we can give each of you an education so you can make your living." We all grew up with that incentive before us, but I am sure that Mother had many depredations because she was determined to make sure we received an education.

Children minded Mother, although J.B. was a problem at first. He decided one morning that he didn't want to go to school; so Mother called my oldest brother, who was nearly grown by that time. She said, "Harry, I want you to take J.B. down to school." So Harry caught J.B., picked him up bodily, and took him to school. The teacher took over from there, and Mother never had any more problems with him. Apparently, he decided that this was a different regime from the one he had left at home. I, too, got one switching when I was little. I forget what sin I had committed, but I had to go and cut the switch and take it to Mother. It wasn't a very bad switching, but it was humiliating, and I've never forgotten it.

# THREE

Interest in medicine seemed to be an inherited tendency in our family. The Governor's interest took the form of homeopathic remedies, but he sent my grandfather for a degree in medicine from the College of South Carolina in Charleston and for postgraduate work in Philadelphia. My aunts, Julia and Katharine were also interested. Julia intended to study medicine, but was diverted. Katharine attended Johns Hopkins to become a nurse, but left to marry John Sedgwick Billings, a New York doctor. Even more than the Hammonds, the Billings had doctors in the family. It was John Shaw Billings who determined that Johns Hopkins Hospital be dedicated to medical education.

Mother, with eight children of her own and with J.B., had a lot of experience with doctoring. Her example of helping with the medical problems of anyone in the neighborhood was the primary influence in my life. There was one old country doctor who came to the house when we really needed him. I remember I disliked the smell of his bag when he opened it because of the medicine it contained. Of course, the doctor was not very often available, so Mother would try to pass on the common sense things that she had learned through experience with her own children. There were some twenty black families on the farm most of the time, and there were a lot of babies and young children. When the babies were sick, the parents brought them up to the house for Mother to see before sending for the doctor.

Mother saved many of the babies on the place. The parents guessed that their babies were sick with diarrhea or "summer complaint," and gave them all kinds of strange remedies. Mother straightened out their diet and told them what she had learned from the doctor for her own children. Sometimes, when a child was cut, the people put cobwebs and soot on the injury, which was supposed to stop the bleeding and keep it from becoming infected. It could hardly have been a worse treatment!

Even on the hottest day in summer the people would keep these poor little children tightly wrapped in the fancy blankets they had saved up to buy. The babies would be sweating and full of nettle rash and hardly able to breathe. Mother took them home and gave them a cooling bath. Many of the babies had thrush, and mother washed out their mouths with boric acid solution, which we used in a variety of ways. When a newborn's umbilical cord came off and there was a little rawness around it, people often put potato leaves on the spot to cure it. One of the remedies for people with high temperature was to cut up onions and put them in a piece of cheesecloth on the forehead. When the mothers started the babies on solid food ... and there was no baby food you could buy ... Mother taught them how to mash up vegetables and begin feeding solid food, instead of having the babies nurse for a year and a half or more. Most of Mother's doctoring involved simple cleanliness and common sense.

When the five oldest of us had the measles, we kept the entire household busy. We were all together in one room, each in an iron crib looking for all the world like animals in small cages. As soon as one of us reached a crisis, the next one came down. Louise capped the climax by getting pneumonia on top of the measles, and then she and Katharine had whooping cough a little later, but I don't know why I never got whooping cough.

I specifically remember two occasions when neighbor women were having babies, and both were having a very bad time. Mother had never studied obstetrics, but she had had babies of her own, and I know she saved the life of at least one of the babies. Mother did so much to take care of people on the farm that I was inspired to study medicine. I was about 13 years old when I realized that I could become a doctor, and soon after that, nearly everyone began to call me "Doc."

Miss Mary Rooney was a white woman from Augusta who was hired to care for me and my brothers and sisters. She was a wonderful nurse, but none of us could say "Miss Rooney," so she became "Shooney" to all of us. She lived at Kathwood and stayed through the births of four or five of the children. When Mother wasn't available, Shooney would sing us to sleep at night. She was wonderfully kindhearted and a devoted friend and companion for fifteen or twenty years; but she went blind as a result of cataracts, and retired with her people in Augusta. Once or twice a year we would be taken there to visit her so she could keep up with our growth.

Hester was the family cook for about 30 years. She had a strenuous life. She lived in a little house in the yard, and she went home for a while each afternoon to relax. The grits that had been water-ground at the mill still had the husks on, so they had to be washed and sifted and cooked on a wood stove in a cold kitchen on winter mornings ... and on very hot summer days. The fire had to be laid and the stove reheated for all three meals. She would come down and wash the hominy at 5:00 in the morning, stoking the wood-stove to fix breakfast. She wasn't a great cook, but she supplied our hungry horde with lots to eat of whatever was available. She fixed the midday meal and prepared dinner at 10:00 at night, if necessary. I can see her now, always wearing her bandana; but Hester was a loner ... a withdrawn and cantankerous person with a great many superstitions. Some mornings she would say she hadn't slept because "the h'ants had been riding her all night." Some of the other black people on the place thought she was a witch because of her formidable looks and her habit of talking to herself. She didn't want anyone to disturb her in her kitchen which was a separate building in the yard. It was rather like the "Black Hole of Calcutta" to us children. Hester had to carry all the food from the kitchen to the house, trying to keep it hot until it got to the table.

On the first Sunday of every month, Hester went to church. We thought it was a great hardship when Hester wasn't there to fix Sunday dinner! I liked to do the cooking, but Louise said that I cheated her because it was much harder to clean up than to cook. I did think the cooking was more fun, even though I had to go out to the kitchen and try to find clean pots to cook in. We must have been immune to the lack of cleanliness, because all the pots had been stored with food residue in them; and by the time I had scrubbed them and cooked in them, the day was pretty well done. On the days that Hester was sick or away, Daddy would sometimes go out through the farm asking every woman he could find to "Go up and help Miss Mary cook today." Of course, Mother would much rather have cooked by herself than to have somebody right out of the cornfield who didn't know how to cook!

Poor Hester died of cancer. She went to the hospital to have all the care that could be given at that time, but afterward she came back and died in her own little house.

# FOUR

*It was real nice at Kathwood. I was at that house every minute
I could get. We loved one another. (After) I'd drive the children
to school in the buggy in the mornings ... I'd get my book and
sit down beside (Mary Hammond's) chair, and she taught me
to read ... a little every day.*

Georgia Davis

There was always a barbecue on the Fourth of July for all the
black people on the plantation. They barbecued three or four hogs
and at least one young goat. There were large barrels of lemonade,
and, of course, bread and rice and all the other things that go with
a barbecue. The party lasted all day, and it was usually a long, hot
day, but you didn't seem to mind the heat as much then.

Of the twenty or so black families who helped on the farm, a
good many of them had never worked for anybody else but our
family. Some of the families simply stayed on after the Civil War,
living on the farm. They had their housing, and each house contained a fireplace with andirons where most of their cooking was
done. There was a handpump in the yard where they got water.
Wages were very small. The workers were paid a dollar a day, but
they got an allowance of corn meal and hominy grits, and a certain
amount of pork was supplied to them. They had a garden space to
grow vegetables, such as collard greens and tomatoes and butter
beans, and so on. They kept chickens, and, if they wanted a cow,
there usually was a place to pasture it.

There were two or three hours in the middle of the day when the
farmhands didn't work because it was too hot. They worked in
gangs and stayed in the fields until sundown. Ten or fifteen women
did the hoeing of the cotton and corn and those crops planted in
rows. In the late afternoon when the people came home from the
fields they would sing, and it was really beautiful. One woman
started off singing and the others followed along, singing all together. The men sang spirituals as they rode their mules back to the barn.

There was always one man we called the yard man. Along with
other chores needing attention, he cut and carried the wood, and
worked in the vegetable garden, and he used a scythe to cut the
grass. We didn't have lawn mowers in those days.

Daddy had a black overseer who truly was one of the most
remarkable people of my childhood. I thought there wasn't anything he couldn't do. His name was Messiah, and he was black,
small, and had a wonderful understanding of animals. In the old
days, the dogs used to get something they called Black Tongue. It

was a vitamin deficiency similar to pellagra in humans. Messiah didn't know why, but he knew how to cure the dogs. He gave them milk and other vitamin-rich foods, and they got well. Each man was assigned the care of one of the mules, but all were supervised by Messiah who made sure that the men didn't abuse the animals. In the Gear House, each mule had its own collar and harness, and the men had to hang them up every afternoon when they got home. Messiah saw that each harness fit each animal, but if a mule had rubbed a raw place on its shoulder, Messiah could cure it.

I remember when I was quite small, Messiah was doing something around the yard at the house. He came up to me and said, "If you don't go in and tell your mother that I want a piece of cake, I am going to turn the house over." Since I believed everything Messiah said, I ran into the house exclaiming to Mother, "Messiah said he is going to turn the house over if you don't give him a piece of cake!"

Mother nearly had hysterics she laughed so hard, but Messiah got his cake! Unfortunately, Messiah got into the bottle heavily in his later years. He was struck by a car on the road and died.

Messiah's wife, Lena, did the laundry for us for a long time. Lena had two very black children and then she had a white-looking blond. Messiah raised her, but I am sure she was not his. Her name was Georgia, and she was my buddy and playmate. She was just three years older than I, but her job on the farm was that of nurse to my brother Keene. Whenever I could entice her away from the squalling baby, we would go out and ride horseback together, or go look for wildflowers or violets in the woods, until we could no longer ignore my mother's irritation at our leaving the baby stranded. The flowers were a peace offering to Mother. Georgia will be ninety-five in October, and when I visit, she and I have a little chat and lots of hugs and kisses. She has returned to Kathwood from Chicago where she worked as housekeeper. She is now living in a house with her daughter, Sadie, and whenever I go south to visit Kathwood, I see Georgia and Sadie. Sadie has never worked for anybody but my sisters. Her son is working our farm at the moment, and he owns his own home and Sadie's and a fairly large farm, and also holds a managerial position with Kimberley-Clark.

Louis, Messiah's son, worked around the house some, too. The house had 11-1/2 foot ceilings and was very hard to heat in the winter. Lots of wood had to be carried upstairs to the fireplaces, and Louis was the one delegated to carry the wood up the stairs and stack it in the hall. One day we heard a tremendous clatter and a call, "Dear Lord, I got religion!" He had thrown the wood down on the steps and run off shouting and waving his hands in the air.

The people would always "seek" before they "got religion," and frequently went around with long and serious faces. They had been told that without religion they were sure to go to Hell. Suddenly, when the Light would shine, that would be it! They dropped everything. It didn't matter where they were or what they were doing.

"I've got it!" they'd shout.

We were invited to Louis' baptism. The baptisms were very important ceremonies and quite impressive. Everyone wore white robes, and they used either the pond down at Kathwood or the very cold water in the creek at Miner's Bridge. The preacher and the chief elders of the church all went into the water, and the converts entered the water to be dipped under. It was important to go all the way under. One old colored woman protested to Grandfather, "That man's gonna drown some of boss' bes' niggahs yet!" After each baptism there would be a church service. I remember Mother gave a huge man a white nightgown to wear for his baptism.

We were invited to most of the weddings and funerals, and Daddy was called on to say a word at most funerals. I remember going to the wedding of a woman who had been Chris' or Keene's nurse. She was all dressed in white, and Mother had given her a white lace curtain for her veil. It was unusual to have a veil in those days, and it spread out behind her on the floor and really looked very beautiful.

One time we were invited to attend what they called "Walk Egypt." The service was designed to represent the twelve tribes of Israel coming home from Egypt. Several of us white people went up to Dead River Church. Among our group was our teacher, Miss Elise Wilson, accompanied by her father, who was a very stout man. When we arrived at the church, we were escorted to the very front pew. Two or three different preachers conducted the ceremony, and there were groups of people dressed in various colored clothing ... green, yellow, and red. The chief preacher carried a large staff. We sat there for a few minutes, and after the preacher got everyone wound up to a high pitch, they began walking around the church and chanting, with the leader beating time with his staff. Just as we got to the peak of the ceremony, our pew collapsed with us! Mr. Wilson, who was a great big man, sat right on the floor. Well, that nearly broke up the service, because the people were so apologetic and so embarrassed that the pew had broken with their guests of honor. After a short interim of confusion, they got reorganized and completed their very impressive ceremony.

# FIVE

Since we were Catholics, we couldn't eat meat on Friday. It seemed always to be a struggle to get a few eggs for our Friday meal, and Daddy went around to all the tenants to try to buy some eggs, if he could find anyone who had them. Sometimes we also had fish that was caught out of the river. There was no fish market ... there was no market at all! Our food came strictly from what grew in the garden or on the farm, and when our chickens produced, we had plenty of eggs.

In addition to the grist mill, we also had a flour mill on the farm, as we had our own wheat for the flour. It made the most delicious biscuits, as I remember. Hester baked enough biscuits in the middle of the day so there would be cold bread for supper, and so she didn't have to bake more than once a day. She always baked at least once a day.

We cured a lot of meat. We butchered a steer and put it in a barrel with salt to make corned beef. In the early winter, around Thanksgiving, they would butcher hogs that had been fattening. They were cured with salt, but if it turned suddenly hot after the hogs had been butchered, it was pretty sad. During the summer the meat didn't last very long, and it would have to be eaten within a day or two.

Making sausage was one of the fun things, because we children were allowed to help. The hog's entrails were carefully cleaned to make the casings for the sausage mixture. If any bubbles of air got into the sausage links, we were allowed to take a pin and prick them. We sat there all day and watched for the bubbles just so we could prick them! They would hang the sausages in the meathouse, and when dried, they lasted for at least two or three months. Sometimes sausages could be packed in a crock with lard on top, and that also preserved them for quite a while.

We were really almost completeley self-sufficient on the farm. When we went to town once or twice a month, we replenished necessary supplies, such as sugar and salt, which we bought in 50-pound bags, and rice, which we bought in 100-pound bags.

For breakfast, if there were eggs, we had them with sausage or bacon, and grits. We always had grits, and we usually had grits for supper, as well. The main meal was in the middle of the day, and we never had a meal in the middle of the day without rice. We had rice and whatever meat there was, with vegetables from the garden. One big chore in the summer was making okra and tomato soup. We grew the okra and tomatoes on the farm, and Mother canned 200 - 300 jars of vegetables and soup mixture, all stored up for the winter. The women on the farm came up to help prepare the five or six bushels of tomatoes and okra, and they worked all day preparing the vegetables and cooking them on the wood stove.

When we finally got an ice box, we had a small one that held a 50 pound block of ice. The food was stored below the ice, and it kept cool for three or four days. Later, Daddy had a larger one especially built with a counterbalanced lid, and we could store quite a bit of food in it. We kept the milk, any leftover food, and butter, meat, and vegetables in the ice box. When we went to town we got a big block of ice ... probably 100 pounds ... and it would last nearly a week, but the only way we could get ice with any regularity was to have the train conductor throw it off the train when it went by over at Brown Hill, about half a mile from the house. Daddy went over in the buggy to meet the train so the ice wouldn't be left to melt on the side of the road. After we got the old Cadillac automobile, we found the luggage rack on the back to be just the right size for a 100-pound block of ice. After church, we would go to the ice house, which was open on Sunday, and buy 100 pounds of ice. We put it on the luggage rack and drove home. Sometimes it seemed that the ice had melted down to 50 pounds by the time we got it into the ice box.

Daddy always wanted ice water to drink. He would come in very hot from supervising the people in the fields, and the one thing he wanted when he got in the house was a pitcher ... not a glass ... but a pitcher of ice water at his end of the table. We actually had two pitchers of ice water at his end of the table. We hesitated a little to chip the ice too much, because it might not last until the next time we went to town.

In the country we girls wore cotton dresses over handmade cotton teddies. In those days, the dresses were almost as short as they are now. They were very simple summer dresses, most of them with no sleeves, so they were easy for Mother to make. A great many of our clothes were hand-me-downs from my two cousins who lived in Columbia. When they outgrew their clothes, we would receive a box in the mail. Then I would hand down whatever was left of my wardrobe to my sister Louise, who was three years younger.

However, I loved to wear pants as much as I could around the farm. My bachelor Uncle Henry offered me a bargain. He proposed that if I would agree not to wear pants again for the rest of my life, he would buy me a very elaborate outfit, and, in addition, he would renew the offer for an indefinite period. But I decided that I would forego that, because I loved to ride horseback. I really was very much of a tomboy while I was growing up, I guess. I loved to climb trees, and we milked cows, and raised two little pet pigs, and I had a flower garden, and later when I was in medical school, I had a vegetable garden.

# SIX

*Our family, being Catholic, was a little set apart from others in the neighborhood. That became apparent early in my life. There was still a great deal of prejudice toward Catholics in the South, and I never had any Catholic friends as I grew up.*

*Emily H. Wilson*

My brother Chris was born on the same day the new school teacher arrived. Miss Elise Wilson was a young lady hired by my father, who, along with two other people from the neighborhood, comprised the Board of Education. As soon as she met Miss Wilson, Mother presented Chris, saying, "Here's another little student for you." All my brothers and sisters attended the neighborhood one-room school house called Brown Hill School, and Miss Wilson taught each of us. We all skipped the eighth grade and went directly into high school, because our grammar school went only through seventh grade.

We usually walked the mile to school. Sometimes we took a shortcut through a neighbor's yard, and in the Spring when his honey bees swarmed, we had quite a time, because you didn't know whether you could get through without being stung. If my brothers went earlier and threw stones at the hives, it was even more of a hazard.

We arrived at school by 9:00 in the morning and stayed until 2:30 in the afternoon, and we brought our lunch. There were 18 to 20 children and seven grades, all in a one-room school with a wood stove in the center. The people who sat on the aisle near the stove were too hot, and the people who sat on the outside near the windows were a little too cold a good part of the time. There were no electric lights, of course, and no central heat, except for the woodstove. There were three of us in my grade, and I sat with one of the girls on a double bench. While we said our lesson, the other students studied theirs. How Miss Wilson organized seven grades in one room with twenty students, I'll never know! She managed with a firm hand, and we were all well-disciplined. If we were caught not studying or if we misbehaved, we were ordered to stand in the corner, or she rapped the ruler across the palm of our hand.

Miss Wilson drove to school with a horse and buggy, and occasionally we rode with her, but sometimes we held a grudge against her. I was once kept after school by a geography lesson. Miss Wilson said,

"Emily, each time you don't know your lesson, this is what we will do. You will have no recess but you will stay in the classroom and study. You won't have time to eat your lunch, and you will stay after school until dark. You will come back at 8:00 tomorrow morning, and then you will begin again until you know the lesson."

I decided it was just easier to learn the lesson, because it seemed there was no way around it. If we made the mistake of telling our mother about any punishment, she would ask, "Well, what did you do?" Between the two of them, my mother and the teacher, we didn't get away with much.

At the end of each school year we had a picnic. It was always a great day! We all went down to the mill by horse and buggy and held the picnic in my father's storage building. The entire school was there, along with all the parents and any friends they cared to invite. Everybody brought something to contribute to the covered dish dinner. We put boards on sawhorses to make tables, and we ate fried chicken and drank lemonade. Before we ate, we swam in the pond, but then we had to wait an hour after eating before swimming again, because everyone said that swimming too soon after eating would give you cramps.

Nearly all of the people who went to school with me were children of small farmers who lived in the neighborhood. Many of their parents had not gone even as far as the seventh grade. Miss Wilson was a miracle worker!

Most of the social life revolved around the churches. There was a very old Baptist church in Beech Island which held all the usual church activities. Quite often I went to this church with my grandfather when I stayed at Redcliffe. We were always invited to the church picnics, and we went to see most of our Baptist cousins baptized. In one way we were more fortunate than they, because their parents were very rigid about activities permitted on Sunday. If our cousins should happen to drive up for a visit while our family was swimming or playing a game of 500, we quickly hid our bathing suits or put away the cards, because our Baptist relatives would have thought we were breaking God's law.

In early Spring, the workers cleaned out the stables where the mules had been kept. They layered the manure with leaves and pine straw to make a compost pile, and they'd let it "cook" until they were ready to plant the cotton. Then the women would take baskets full of the compost and spread it along the deep furrows for the cotton. In our sandy soil, that was great nourishment for the young plants.

At the same time that they cleaned out the stables, they killed so many rats that there were baskets full of carcasses! Somebody jokingly said, "You know, Doc, those rat skins would be worth at least ten cents apiece." So Louise and Harry and I decided we would go into business, and we began to skin the rats and tack up the hides. Harry found a black youngster who would do the work for him on commission, but Louise and I did our own. By the time we got around to the last of them, we had to wear bandages over our noses. We didn't sell one of those skins, and we never tried that again.

Another summer Louise and I took over the chore of milking the cows. We had rather unreliable help at the time, and we thought it was a great frolic to get our three or four cows in from the field, milk them, and take care of them.

We spent many summer afternoons swimming with friends in the mill pond. We hitched a horse to a one-horse wagon, put on our bathing suits and rode down to spend the afternoon. Always for my birthday and for Katharine's, the favorite way to celebrate was a swimming party. Her birthday was July 11th, and mine July 8th, but it never failed to rain on the 8th of July, so we began to move the party to Katharine's birthday. It was just as apt to storm on the 11th of July, but we celebrated together, anyway.

One of our most wonderful summers happened when Daddy rented a house in Beaufort, South Carolina, right on the water, and we spent most of that summer there. Of course, Daddy couldn't stay with us because of the farm, but he did come down for occasional weekends. He bought crates of chickens for 15 cents apiece and sent them down on the train, again with the help of his railroad buddies. We hailed the local fishermen to sell us shrimp and seafood for the table.

We were about five or six children at that time, and Mother took the two maids to Beaufort with us. Daddy had bought a used Cadillac early in the Spring, and, Patterson, the husband of one of the maids, was our driver. After we arrived, Patterson was asked to put the car in a garage. However, he wanted to show the car off, so he drove down the street in front of the hotel, but when he tried to turn the car around, he drove the back wheels over the sea wall in front of the hotel. The front wheels were in the air and the back wheels were hanging over the sea wall. Patterson was frantic, because the tide was coming in, and he hurried to find some help. Finally he gathered nearly everyone in the town of Beaufort, and after some false starts, they literally carried the car around to a break in the seawall and back to solid ground.

# SEVEN

In the early days we rode in the buggy, or we rode horseback. One buggy didn't hold many of our family, so I had to learn to be an outrider pretty early. Unfortunately, none of my brothers cared about horses or liked to ride. Harry, my oldest brother, was given a small stallion with a wonderful gait, but the horse was a mean little devil. If you went to catch him, he would chase you around with his teeth bared. The minute Harry got on him, he was thrown off, but that horse soon learned that I would stay on him, no matter what!

I rode a great deal up at Redcliffe. Aunt Julia was an avid horse-woman, and my uncle had raised four young saddlehorses there. When I first began to ride, I was put on the horse, and someone held a lead line. I remember one really large, very gentle, draft horse. I think it was the first time I was allowed to ride by myself. They put me up, and my legs stuck straight out because her back was so wide. I was determined to ride down the hill to visit my cousins who lived nearby. Part way down the hill, I decided I needed a switch because the horse wasn't going fast enough to suit me. I slid off and cut the switch; but when I tried to remount, I could hardly reach the stirrups with my hand, let alone my foot. Taking her by the bridle, I led the horse to a ledge so that I could mount from the high side; but she was very contrary, and I ended up leading her the rest of the way down the hill.

That day I had used a saddle, but Father had a perfect phobia about stirrups. A child in the neighborhood had been thrown, and, when his foot caught in the stirrup, he was dragged and killed. Therefore, when I got a little horse of my own ... I was about ten, I guess ... I rode with just a blanket strapped on the horse. Fortunately, she was small, so I could mount by jumping up from the ground. It certainly taught me how to stay on a horse. Once, I even tried to ride one of the calves. My brother and one of the black boys were leading the calf and thought they were going to keep it going quietly, but the calf began to run and buck, and off I went!

One of the horses my uncle had raised at Redcliffe was called Willis. He was a tall and very handsome horse. Finally, one day I was allowed to ride Willis down to the millpond where we swam. When my uncle lifted me into the saddle, he warned, "Now, if you sit down too heavily on this horse, he will buck and throw you off." So I stood in my stirrups all the way to the pond and all the way back. I must have weighed all of sixty pounds, and I don't think Willis would have known whether I was sitting on him or not.

Later on when I was in grammar school, there were groups of young people who got together, and, under the chaperonage of Aunt Julia, rode out in the evening to have a picnic, returning after dark. Somehow, these excursions gave us the feeling we had participated in an adventure.

Of course, Mother tried to take us to church every Sunday in Augusta as often as she could. We had a pair of horses and a "surrey with a fringe on top." We left right after breakfast in the morning, because it was an all-day trip. We had to cross the Savannah River at the Sand Bar Ferry, and the length of the trip depended on whether the ferry was on the Georgia side or the South Carolina side when we arrived at the river. We began to hoot for the ferryman as soon as we were within a half mile of the ferry, hoping he would wait on the South Carolina side. The approach to the ferry frequently was deep in mud, and sometimes we had to get out in our good clothes to push the surrey onto the ramp. The ramp at the approach to the ferry was some sort of a flexible metal, and the horses didn't much like it. Sometimes they acted up and refused to step on it, and it took some cajoling to get them to cooperate. Howston, the ferryman, held onto a rope while the horses were driven onto the ferry. The current carried the ferry across to the other side, and during the crossing, Howston dipped a bucket in the river to water the horses so that they would be fresh when they got to town.

We knew only one or two of the families who attended the Sacred Heart Church in Augusta. Occasionally, we were invited to stay for midday dinner after Mass, but there was no real intimacy, probably because we lived so far from town. We often had sandwiches or some sort of picnic which we ate on the way home to keep us quiet. If the weather was bad, or the river in flood, or if some of us were sick, Mother would say the Mass prayers at home. We all assembled, and Mother and Daddy invited whomever the help was at the time to join us, but I'm afraid they usually preferred to keep working.

My father's first automobile was that second-hand Cadillac. When we began going to church in the Cadillac, we had to push it out of the mud just as often as we'd had to push the buggy. It had two front seats and two back seats and wooden wheels with tires and no bumpers. The driver had to look at the gear shift box to be certain he had put the lever in the correct section to make the car go forward. Daddy had a hard time trying to learn how to drive it. Once when he tried to turn the car around, instead of going backward as he planned, the car went forward and smashed into the large chinaberry tree in the yard. One wooden wheel hit the tree and collapsed. They got the wheel fixed, and by the time I was eleven, I had learned how to drive. I was hardly tall enough to see over the steering wheel, but I could drive down to the mill to go swimming.

Later, after the ferry closed down, they built another road, called the Swamp Road, which was full of mud holes. If the river was flooded, you couldn't get through, so we were sometimes completely isolated from Augusta. About two years out of three the river flooded out of its banks. The worst part was that the flooding destroyed so many crops in the low-lying areas. Fortunately, my father didn't do much farming in what they called the Swamp, but some of the people in Beech Island did. They lost all their crops, along with any livestock they had ... mules, horses, pigs and cattle ... unless they got them out ahead of time. Of course, some very rich soil was built up that way. They have built a dam up above Augusta now, so they don't have that flooding anymore.

In 1916, when I was twelve, my parents, my brother and I drove up to Augusta because we had seen something strange in the sky. We didn't realize what it was at first, but what we had seen was the reflection of the flames of the burning city twelve miles away from Kathwood. The fire was located in probably the oldest residential part of Augusta ... in the lower part of the city. It was a terrible inferno. We got there fairly late and found that a lot of the city had already burned.

Our friend, Katharine Moore, remembered the fire vividly, because she was living in Augusta at the time. Katharine was a family friend, a single child who spent a good deal of time at Kathwood. My Uncle Henry had given her grandfather a stag party when he reached his 100th birthday, and Katharine was the only female invited ... she was three years old. To Katharine, the Augusta fire was one of the most memorable events of her early life. Her family had to evacuate the city with as many possessions as they could manage.

# EIGHT

There was no high school within easy commuting distance, so when I graduated from the Brown Hill School, I was sent to Baltimore to Mount St. Agnes to attend high school. It was located in the village of Mt. Washington, but it's gone now. Mount St. Agnes was operated by the Sisters of Mercy, and Mother and both of my aunts had gone there to school. My great aunt had been a nun there, so I got a scholarship. I had turned thirteen in July and went to Baltimore in September. I was at St. Agnes for a year and was very homesick most of the time. It was, I think, as much the weather, being cold and snowy, as missing my brothers and sisters. My aunt, Mrs. Scrivener, was Mother's sister and lived in Baltimore. She came out to Mt. Washington to visit me perhaps as often as once a month. Occasionally, I rode the streetcar to her home to spend the weekend. Learning where to get on and off the streetcars and trains was a new experience for a country girl. I remember that one time my aunt went to a big DAR meeting in Washington. I went along with her, but for some reason she returned home early. By the time I returned to Baltimore it was late at night, and I landed at Camden Yard Station instead of Mt. Royal Station. I didn't know quite where I was and had to find the correct streetcar in unfamiliar territory.

Mother and both of my aunts were musical, especially one aunt who was talented enough to have been a concert pianist. I was scheduled to take music lessons, but, although I loved music, I had no ear for it and barely got beyond the scales. I loved to listen to the nun who taught music. She had a beautiful singing voice and had studied piano at Peabody. As a treat, I was allowed to listen to her play the piano every now and then. She tried hard to interest me in the piano, but I usually smuggled a book into the practice rooms; and when I was supposed to be practicing, I read, so I didn't make much progress.

The school itself was a very large brick building and was very self-sufficient. There was a chapel and a cemetery for the nuns, and very pretty grounds on top of a hill. The nuns had their own quarters and their own meals. There was a large dormitory with at least 30 girls on each floor. We each had a small cubicle where we kept our clothes and undressed for the night, drawing the curtain across the opening for privacy. Our beds were placed in the big open ward, and we had to be undressed and in bed by a specified time. A little later one of the nuns came along to be sure we were in bed and not out on the fire escape smokng.

24

I studied the usual things: English and algebra and religion. I'd had little exposure to religious studies before I went to Mt. St. Agnes, and I think that was one reason I was sent there. Each day began with Chapel, and on holidays and feast days they had beautiful music in the Chapel. The nuns, on specials days, wore a white robe with a little train over their black habits, and it was impressive to see them all march up to the altar for Communion. We had a little extra foodstuffs on these feast days, which made them more special, too. I remember my first taste of rhubarb. We didn't have it in South Carolina, and in Baltimore we were served it once or twice a week. I might have liked it better had it been served in a pie, but it was served stewed. However, we were taught to eat everything on our plates, because of the "starving Armenians."

There were several special occasions at Mt. St. Agnes. On May Day, we had a procession to a statue of the Madonna. We all carried flowers, and we marched down the hill to a grotto. My aunt had brought me some lilacs to carry, but unfortunately, by the time we got to the end of the march, my lilacs were all wilted.

I remember the last day at school before we left for the summer. We stood in a circle and held hands and sang "Old Lang Syne." But, somehow everything still seemed very foreign, and I didn't have any close friends. Even though the Spring was beautiful, and there were flowers all in bloom, I didn't like city life, and I still had in mind that I would be a country doctor.

Since we had train passes available because of my father's connections, I went home to Kathwood on the train. It was an overnight trip from Baltimore, and I had a Pullman section. Although we got coach passes, we had to write ahead to get special permits for Pullman spaces because it cost extra money. If we notified them in advance, the train would stop at Kathwood. I had told the conductor, who knew my father, that I wanted to get off there. I suppose he forgot, because, as the train passed Kathwood with the family standing out waiting for me and waving, the train passed through the station! My parents were irritated with me, because they had to go all the way to Augusta to meet me.

I would probably have returned to Mt. St. Agnes the following year, except that my Uncle Keene, who was a priest, got me a scholarship to St. Genevieve's in Ashville, North Carolina. I was happy not to be going quite as far away as Baltimore, although Ashville was an all-day train trip. I got a train in Augusta at five o'clock in the morning, and arrived in Spartanburg, where there was a layover of two or three hours before the train took off for the mountains. Fortunately, I had an uncle who lived in Spartanburg, so he came down to the train to meet me. He took me to his home for lunch and back to the train. At Tryon, an extra engine was attached for the trip up the mountain to Ashville, where we arrived at three o'clock in the afternoon.

St. Genevieve's was a small school comparatively. An old hotel in a beautiful spot in the mountains had been converted into the school. It overlooked Mt. Pisgah and some of the pretty scenery around Ashville. In the Spring they placed big rocking chairs on the porches. These chairs had one enlarged arm which could be used as a desk surface, and when the weather improved in the Spring, study hall was held on the porch.

I was required to take everything with me, from sheets and towels to underclothes, and had spent a boring part of the summer sewing name tags on everything. I didn't take but a couple of dress-up dresses, because I would be wearing a uniform. Included in my large trunk were union suits. We wore hightop shoes and union suits, and the union suit came down the leg, and the stockings were pulled over the union suit. The hightop shoes met the union suit on the leg. It was quite a process to get it all maneuvered so there wasn't a lump around the ankle. I disliked the uniform and got awfully tired of wearing the same clothes every day. Fortunately, we didn't have to worry about being stylish.

Our lives were very regimented. For instance, there was even a schedule for our twice-weekly baths. One bit of freedom that I always enjoyed was the Saturday afternoon hike in the country-side. It was a great change from our incarceration on the grounds of the school. I missed not being able to ride, but there were no horses at St. Genevieve's. Once or twice a year, the school held a dance where we girls danced with each other. No boys were invited, although there was a school for boys almost across the road. One of our girls discovered that she could meet one of their boys in secret, engaging in a little clandestine flirtation, and she was nearly expelled for her transgression.

The nuns at St. Genevieve's were in a French Order, and most of the nuns were French, although a few were Irish. The nuns were very patriotic, and we were kept thoroughly informed of the progress of the First World War. I was sorry that I wasn't older and a graduate nurse, because I would have loved to serve overseas. Once a week there were lectures in French which we were required to attend. I finally was able to understand most of it, but I never did speak it very well. One nun ate at each dining table to help our French conversation. This practice was valuable because it allowed the students to get to know the nuns as people. The nun who sat at our table was Irish, and was a very bright woman who taught history. She was the sister of the Lord Mayor of Cork; and near the end of the war, he went on a hunger strike, starving himself to death in a protest during one of the early Irish freedom fights.

Those of us who sat at her table had become very close to her, and we shared her sadness.

I received a wonderful education in my three years at St. Genevieve's. I graduated from high school in a class of eight. At that time I was very anxious to go to Johns Hopkins Medical School. I was sixteen, and I was very ambitious!

# NINE

Knowing of my need to enter a pre-med course before I could enter Johns Hopkins, my Aunt Loulie offered, "Doc, why don't you come up to Baltimore and live with me? You can go to Goucher for pre-med, and it's right here close to Hopkins."

I accepted Aunt Loulie's invitation and returned to Baltimore, registering for classes at Goucher, but, even though I didn't like the city, I found some of it interesting. Aunt Loulie and I would go shopping down at the Lexington Market, which really was a wonderful treat. She would do her week's grocery shopping and haggle her way around the market, which I thought was fun. Sometimes the man across the aisle would call across and say, "Listen, I'll sell you the same thing for two cents off."

Goucher at that time was downtown near North Avenue and only four blocks from where Aunt Loulie lived, so I walked back and forth to school every day. I attended Goucher as a day student, but I think that perhaps I missed a lot by being a day student. I got along very well at school, considering that I had come right out of the country. Of course, I was bewildered to begin with, because I was in a class of thirty or forty girls who'd had very different high school experiences. I had a hard time with chemistry and sciences, because I hadn't studied much science in high school.

One of my courses was Political Science. I took it as extra credit, because I was taking several other sciences for pre-med. After she called the roll on the very first day, the professor said,

"Miss Hammond, will you stay after class?"

I thought, "What in the world have I done so soon?" After class I very shakily approached her desk, and she asked,

"Did you come from South Carolina?"

"Yes," I answered.

"Well, I wrote about your great-grandfather's life for my Ph.D. thesis."

"Well," I breathed to myself, "Maybe I'll pass one class."

Unfortunately, that was the only bright spot in my academic year at Goucher, because at that time, Hopkins required a reading knowledge of scientific German. When I went to my first German class I was completely overwhelmed because all of the girls in the class had studied German in high school and were far ahead of me. Maybe the worst thing was that they had been taught the German script, which I had hardly even seen. I decided that German was a subject I just couldn't master, and that killed any idea I'd had of going to Johns Hopkins!

The Medical College of Georgia in Augusta, twelve miles from home, was the obvious and convenient second choice for my medical education. Therefore, to complete my pre-med studies, I decided to change to the University of Georgia in Athens. Again, I lived with distant relatives, paying board, and walking about four blocks to school. I had a delightful time from that point of view. While I was there, I helped to found the Alpha Alpha Chapter of Phi Mu sorority at the University of Georgia. (Recently, the Annapolis Alumnae Chapter had a dinner at which they honored me for more than 50 years of service and 70 years of membership in Phi Mu by making a donation in my name to the Phi Mu Foundation.)

Academic standards were different in those days. A student was required to complete only two or three years of college, depending on whether one could complete the required sciences. There was no liberal arts requirement, so I took four sciences at the University of Georgia: chemistry, physics, zoology, astronomy and more French. It was a very heavy course load because I had laboratory in one subject or the other nearly every afternoon, and then I had to do the regular study hours in addition. Again, chemistry was a very difficult subject for me. It is such an intangible subject, and there was nothing that I could put my finger on, as it were. The young post-graduate student who was in charge of the laboratory said to me,

"There's no use for you to go to medical school. You're not going to be able to pass because you don't know any chemistry. You really don't!"

It was nearly impossible for a woman to be accepted as a serious student, and so it was difficult to receive any attention from the staff or the professors. The chemistry professor was an old man who had been a friend of my grandfather's at the University of Georgia. Although he had to teach women in his classes, the professor believed that it wasn't fair to call on women students because if they didn't know the answer to his question, they would be embarrassed.

# TEN

Although I admit to wondering a few times if I would really be successful, I never lost sight of my goal of becoming a country doctor. My parents were cooperative, but not eager, for me to try it, and occasionally it must have been a hardship for them. My Uncle Henry had become a judge by this time and was quite prominent in Augusta. After I completed pre-med, Uncle Henry agreed to become my sponsor at the Medical College of Georgia because the only way I could get into medical school was to have some connection to Georgia. I registered at medical school as his niece, but Uncle Henry didn't think that the situation would last very long because he was convinced I wouldn't stay the course. The tuition was $200 per year in those days, but it was a lot of money for us. I don't remember who paid it now, but I didn't have to work for it. I think that if I'd had to have a job in addition to commuting to classes I might not have made it.

At that time the family owned a little Ford touring car, and I was allowed to use it every day to drive back and forth to classes. After about the second year, my sister Katharine attended high school in Augusta, and she rode with me. Katharine would undertake to read me some of my neurology assignment while I drove, but frequently the vocabulary was a little over her head. We were given long textbook assignments, sometimes 40 - 60 pages a day, along with everything else.

There were times when the commute into Augusta was difficult because floods would wash out the roads, and we'd have to drive the long way around. Coming home one night from school in 1925 or 1926, Katharine was driving. I'd been late getting out of school, and it was about 8:00 p.m. and dark. Road crews had been working on the road, but they had left a big stump lying right in the middle of the track. Katharine didn't see it, and we hit the stump square on. My head cracked the windshield, I got a big knot on my head, and the car was completely disabled. We had to walk about a mile home, and by the time we got to Kathwood, the family were all sitting around the table having dinner. Katharine suggested,

"Now, Doc, you go in first, because when they see that knot on your head, they will feel so sorry for you that they won't fuss with me about wrecking the car!" Daddy had to find a wrecker to pull the car home.

I began my medical school class with two other women students, both of whom were from Armenia. How they ever got from Armenia to Augusta, Georgia, I don't know. One of them dropped out the first year, and the other dropped out the second year. The boys teased,

"You know, we'd thought we'd lose you in the third year, and here you are still with us."

I retorted, "Well, I'm sorry to disappoint you, and I'd like to be accommodating; but I'm not going to quit!"

The first year we were thrown into the Dissecting Hall. It sort of weeded out the men from the boys, I suppose. A lot of men students fainted, but I was not going to faint if I'd had to be propped up with starch! That would have been the end of my career, I am sure. We wore lab gowns, but even so, our clothes got to smell very much of formaldehyde. Somehow you couldn't get the smell off your hands. We were working on human cadavers, and there were four of us sharing one cadaver. Our group had a female. Two of us would work on each side, two taking the lower and two taking the upper sections of the body. After three months, we traded positions, working an entire year on one cadaver. It was very slow, because we had to do the different layers of the skin, for instance, and dissect from there all the way through. I had seen animals being cut up ... pigs and cattle and all that, but the first two years of medicine were very difficult. However, we had a remarkably good professor in Dissecting Hall. I helped him dissect a special duct in the neck which he wanted to write about. There was a lot of theory in the first two years, but I was looking forward to saving people instead of dissecting them. I would hate to go through it again, and I was glad when it was behind me.

Occasionally when the professor left the room, some of the boys would start to fight, throwing around the fat and tissue. I must have had a strong instinct for survival because I realized I couldn't permit them to see me flinch, or I might become a target myself. One day after a particularly rough morning in the Dissecting Hall, I went out to lunch with some of the male students. Somebody ordered grilled cheese, and they began to compare it to what we'd been studying ... subcutaneous fat!

During the first year of medical school, we were each issued a box of bones to take home to study for Anatomy because in Dissecting Hall we dissected only the soft tissues and not the bones. My brothers and sisters were sure there were ghosts connected with the box of bones, and complained that I would frighten them with the skull or with the long bones. Actually, I didn't do it intentionally, but Julian still teases me about it.

I wasn't an "A" student. I was about in the middle of the class, I guess, although I made an "A" in physiological chemistry. One great problem was that I couldn't draw anything. We sat for hours looking at slides through the microscope, and we were required to reproduce what we saw on drawing paper kept beside the micro-scope. Fortunately, one of the students was a good friend, and he would sketch the background for me, and then I would put in the colors of the cells. It was a great struggle for me to draw anything, and I still have no idea of how to produce a drawing.

Classes were from 9:00 to 5:00, and when I came home in the afternoon, I would need to do something completely different to wash it all out of my mind. In the Fall or Spring while there was still daylight I would work in the garden. I had both a vegetable garden and a flower garden, and I had some very nice things growing. My other diversion was to ride horseback when I got home; but in the winter months, Mother didn't want me to ride alone in the dark. Harry, who despised even the thought of a horse, dutifully accompanied me, using our only saddle while I rode bareback.

One day when I came home during my third year of medical school, Mother said, "Doc, we have a surprise for you. Go out and see what is hitched to the tree out there."

It was a new horse. I was in the midst of chemistry at that time, so I called her "C2," the name of the carbon atom that had almost defeated me in college. I became very fond of her.

I remember at one of the conferences they discussed diagnosing tuberculosis, and in those days, there was no advanced science enabling doctors to diagnose many diseases. A guinea pig was injected with some fluid from the patient's chest. If the guinea pig developed TB, you knew that your diagnosis was correct, but it took about six weeks to get a diagnosis.

The professor asked me, "And how could you hurry the test to get the report sooner?"

"Well," I said, "I guess you could get a guinea pig that was kind of sick, anyhow."

The class burst out laughing! The correct answer was that you treated the guinea pig with radiation to lower its resistance. I guess I hadn't studied that part correctly.

By our second year, we began to go into the wards under super-vision to observe actual patients who had some of the conditions we had read about in the medical books. We were not allowed to touch the patients, but we were to attempt a diagnosis by observa-tion only. When we were studying ascites in the abdomen, we went into the ward to see one or two patients who had both edema and ascites. We came to the bed of a woman patient who had a greatly enlarged abdomen. They asked me what I thought her con-dition was, and I said,

"Well, it sort of looks like ascites."

Again everybody burst out laughing, because the woman was

32

nine months pregnant! I didn't mind making the mistake, and I was able to laugh with them, which was lucky for me.

Another funny thing happened in my second year. There was going to be a small community horse show in Beech Island. It was the kind of show which demonstrated the skill of the rider rather than the quality of the horse. I was getting ready to ride in the show, but I had a little boil on my rear end which was very uncomfortable. There were no antibiotics in those days, but I was determined to ride. That boil got to be pretty big and very painful, and finally it had to be lanced. When I returned to classes, I took a pillow to use on the wooden stool in the laboratory. When the boys learned the reason for the pillow, it became a wonderful joke, and I became known as "The Pillow" for quite a while.

Of course, there weren't too many chances for a social life, but I did have some fun as I was going along in addition to trying to do some real work. Fortunately I was invited to the fraternity dances at the Medical College, and my boyfriend, Tup, and I were dating. I remember one dress that I thought I just couldn't live without. It was a beautiful green velvet dress with a big ostrich plume on one side. I wanted it for one of the dances at the Medical College, and although money was very scarce in the family at the time, Mother saw that I got it. I'm convinced that she was anxious that I not appear too masculine, since there had been some discussion in the family that "Emily might wear derby hats and smoke cigars upon becoming a doctor."

Every now and then I would invite some of my classmates home with me for our lunch break, and on weekends some of them would come down and go fishing in the pond. All the while I was in medical school I left a toothbrush at Redcliffe. Sometimes I went to Redcliffe to spend the night after a late dance or party, and Aunt Julia might not realize I was there until I came down in the morning. Aunt Julia spoiled me, I guess.

I'll never forget the first operation we were allowed to observe. The surgery was on a child with a harelip, and the doctors were to operate on the inside of the mouth. In those days hospitals had no air conditioning in the operating room, or anywhere else, for that matter. An open cone of ether was used to anesthetize the patient. Our class, all done up in white lab coats, filed into the operating room. The operation was very bloody, and the heat, the ether, and the sight of this child having the inside of his mouth worked on was just too much. After a while, one by one, six or seven of the men began to sneak to the door, and two of them passed out completely on the floor! Everyone watched me closely, expecting me to pass out; but I propped myself up somehow. It was very interesting, and I was there because I was interested.

We performed surgery on dogs for practice, and as much as I love animals, I found this very interesting, also. Now when I look back on it, I don't know how I could have done it. If we wanted a dog instead of a cat to use for surgery ... cats were supplied by the hospital ... we had to provide our own dog. We got stray dogs, from the pound, not our pets, of course. You would take perfectly good healthy dogs and do the surgery ... a G-section or some other major surgery; and you cared for them and hoped they would survive. One student did the anesthetic and the other student did the surgery. The animals were taken care of by attendants on the top floor of the medical college building where they were fed and given humane treatment; but you would hear them whining, and that was pretty hard for me. I don't think many of the boys noticed.

When I was in my junior year, my sister and two of my brothers got viral pneumonia. I obtained a leave of absence for about a month to go home to help care for them. They were seriously ill; in fact, my professor of medicine came out to consult with my family doctor regarding their treatment. He said that Katharine was the one in the worst condition, and he was concerned that she might go into congestive heart failure during the night. His recommendation was that she be bled, and he turned to my father and said,

"Of course, Emily can take care of that in an emergency."

My heart sank to my toes, and I thought, "Oh, no!"

Fortunately for me, Daddy said, "No, we are going to get somebody else out here." As it was, Katharine developed empirema of the lung, requiring surgical drainage.

Our family physician was requested to come out to Kathwood to spend the night. In the middle of the night, Chris developed a terrible pain in his side. The others had started with the same symptoms, so we were convinced that he, too, was coming down with pneumonia. Before the doctor left the house the next morning, he examined Chris again and announced, "Oh, he's got acute appendicitis!" I went with Chris in the ambulance and was with him when he had surgery because Mother had to stay with the other children. It seems strange now, but we were all so relieved that Chris had appendicitis instead of pneumonia. Pneumonia was an extremely serious disease before the antibiotics that were developed so much later.

Before I graduated from medical school, the State of Georgia had begun to construct a bridge across the Savannah River designed to shorten the commute to Augusta by at least ten miles. The contractors had nearly finished the bridge except for about 30 feet of the approach. Apparently the State of Georgia wouldn't let the contractor finish the bridge, because then they would have had to settle his bill. The bridge had been hanging there unopened for some time. The contractor contacted one of our crowd, saying that if we would nail the boards on the decking, he would leave all the equipment for us to do it. About twenty-five of us ... both men and women ... got together one night and made a big party of it. We nailed on the decking, and we held an unofficial bridge opening in the middle of the night. We drove across the bridge and into Augusta and rode up and down Broad Street, blowing our horns and celebrating. From then on we could commute back and forth on this shorter, more direct, and much better road to Augusta.

I graduated from the Medical College of Georgia in 1927, the only woman in my class, and the second woman to graduate from the medical school.

Graduation was held in the evening during the first part of June at one of the theaters. We all marched up to get our diplomas in our caps and gowns. I was wearing a very pretty pink chiffon dress which didn't show at all under my black academic gown. My Uncle Henry, who had sponsored my education, had extensive gardens with lots of beautiful flowers at his place outside of Augusta. He brought me two big baskets of Pink Radiance roses, which were placed on either side of the stage during the graduation ceremonies. I walked up the same steps as the boys to receive my diploma, but I really floated. It had been a long struggle, and I could hardly believe it had happened at last!

The whole family attended the graduation, and afterwards we went to the country club, where there was a dance, and finally, I could show off my pretty pink dress. My uncle and his lady friend, my mother and father, and my boyfriend, Tup, were all there. The older generation didn't stay long at the Ball, but Tup and I had a wonderful evening, and we danced late into the night.

The very next day, we students had to sit for the two-day State Board Examinations! That was a real nightmare, but we got through it by coaching each other.

I wasn't able to learn whether I had passed or not, because the morning after the two days of examinations, I left to drive up to Canada with my priest uncle and my mother.

Uncle Keene had a nice Buick. Although he and my mother both drove, I did most of the driving, and we stopped several times on the way, reaching Montreal two days after we started. We arrived about lunchtime, and after lunch, Mother and I decided we would take a nap. We both slept right through until the next morning! I was absolutely exhausted mentally and physically, and I think that since Mother had been living through my struggles with me, she was just as exhausted as I was.

We proceeded to have a very nice time sightseeing in Montreal, and afterward we took a beautiful drive along the St. Lawrence River on the way from Montreal to Quebec. It was the Feast of Corpus Christi, and all the villages along the road were decorated with flowers. My uncle knew the Chaplain for the Ursuline Convent where Montcalm's skull and other relics were kept. Uncle Keene was given the Chaplain's quarters for our two or three day visit, and they put Mother and me in what had been Montcalm's headquarters during the Battle of Quebec.

We were gone for two weeks, and I was praying that there would be good news when we returned. Thank God, the news was good! I had passed the State Boards.

# ELEVEN

*I did not escape the widespread prejudice against women doctors ... it was made very clear to me.*
Emily H. Wilson

Before I graduated from med school, I had applied for an internship at the Willingford Hospital in Augusta, a 100-bed hospital for women and children. Although the Board of Governors included some of my Augusta cousins, my application was rejected. It was decided that a woman resident wouldn't do. However, there was a new hospital in Savannah: Central Georgia Railroad Hospital. It had opened the first of July, and I secured a firm commitment for a job there. The hospital had only about sixty beds and was paid for by the employees of the Central Georgia Railroad. They paid a certain amount of dues, and then were entitled to free medical attention at the hospital. Naturally, most of those patients were men.

The Chief Surgeon was Dr. Craig Barrow, and he was a friend of a mutual friend. While taking pre-med in Athens, I had become acquainted with Mrs. Barrow, who had friends in the city. She had come from quite a prominent family in Savannah and thought she was only a little less important than God! I thought we had become pretty well acquainted, so it was a surprise to me that, after I was working at Central Georgia Hospital, she never spoke to me, and I was never invited to their house the entire year I was at the hospital.

The head nurse, a Miss Moyer, had worked at the French Hospital in New York, and she was quite a disciplinarian ... a very rigid and difficult girl. Even though I was by then a doctor, I was not quite good enough to sit at her dining table. Her assistant and the resident, when he took meals there, were welcome at her table, but I sat with some of the nurses. The resident, Reed Broderick, lived in Savannah, but he had a room at the hospital because he had to be on duty much of the time. Reed was a nice young fellow, and I became very fond of him.

When the Southern Medical Association had a big meeting in Savannah, I went to the seminars. Dr. Barrow usually gave a party for the members of the Association at his house, but I was not invited because it was a stag party. Reed and I had arranged to attend the seminar together the morning after the party, but I waited and waited, and he didn't appear. Finally I knocked on his door, and asked him if he were going to the seminar. He still didn't answer. I opened his door just a crack, and he groaned "Oh, my

God! I have a terrible head!" He had never before tasted champagne and apparently had gulped it like ginger ale. I don't think he ever made it out of bed that day, and I was somewhat glad I hadn't gone to the party.

My job at the Central Georgia Railroad Hospital entailed taking the medical histories and performing physical examinations on all of the patients that were admitted, and I was on call nearly 24 hours a day except for one weekend a month. My pay was $50 per month and a pass to go home on that free weekend. I had a room with bath and meals in the hospital, so I really had no expenses except for uniforms. Mother decided that I ought to look professional, but feminine, so she and I designed a white skirt and a jacket, and she and a sewing woman made up several uniforms for me.

Not long after I arrived at Central Georgia Railroad Hospital, the lab technician and the x-ray technician were called home because of family illnesses. Added to my duties, then, were the duties of the pharmacist, lab technician, and x-ray technician for the hospital. There were periods when it was very strenuous because of interrupted sleep. A great many tonsilectomies were performed in those days, and often in the middle of the night I was called to the floor to stop a patient's post-operative bleeding. Another part of my job was to sit at night with any dying patient, so all in all, there was a good deal of pressure.

In the afternoon from 2:00 to 4:00 we held Outpatient Clinic for the local employees, and it was my responsiblity to be there under the supervision of one of the staff people. It was very hot, and we had no air conditioning. Savannah in the summer is one of the most uncomfortable places in the world. After every thunderstorm it got hotter instead of cooler, and my nice fresh uniform would be completely wilted by suppertime.

In February, my Mother came down to Savannah for a visit. Mother was very agile and active at that time. We did some sightseeing, and that evening we went to the movies. As she stepped off a little step at the end of the aisle, she fell and broke her hip. She was in her early fifties, which is quite young for such an event; but she'd had eight children, and they didn't know about calcium therapy in those days.

We took her back to the hospital, and Dr. Barrow set the hip. He placed Mother in a cast from under her arms all the way to her ankle. She was at the Railroad Hospital for two months, and it was a terrible ordeal for her, because she was completely immobile and extremely uncomfortable. It wasn't too much easier for Daddy, because the children at home came down with measles, and my father was absolutely panicky with both Mother and me away. Although the doctor had come from Augusta to see the sick children, all he said was, "It's measles, all right." Messiah came up to the house and helped Daddy nurse Chris, Julian, and Keene through a hard time.

Mother's hip just didn't seem to be healing. Once when she tried to turn over she fell out of bed. The doctors were sure that the fall shook the joint loose, but I remain convinced it was never properly set in the first place. She went back to Kathwood, walking with the help of a cane, but the hip never did heal. The next year when I was at Johns Hopkins and Mother came up to visit, I took her to see Dr. Baer, who was considered one of the foremost orthopedists in the world.

He exclaimed, "Mrs. Hammond, you are walking on will power alone! You don't have any bony union."

Dr. Baer explained to her that it would soon be possible to replace the whole joint, but the procedure hadn't yet been perfected. For the rest of her life Mother had a lot of pain and was somewhat handicapped. One leg was about an inch shorter than the other, so she had to have one shoe built up and she used a cane, but it didn't seem that she was slowed down very much.

I remained at Central Georgia Railroad Hospital until July, but when I was offered a second year of employment without an increase in my salary I refused the offer, declaring, "If you don't think I'm worth more now than when I came here, I can't stay."

# TWELVE

I went home to Kathwood where I sat for at least a month without any prospect of another job. My father was nearly beside himself. He said, "I knew this would happen, Doc! We made such an effort to help you through medical school, and here you sit at home! We need you to work!"

I spent my time answering ads in the Journal of the American Medical Association. Finally, I was offered two positions, one in Morgantown, West Virginia, and the other in a big general hospital in Portland, Maine. I also learned of a rather vague possibility of a position doing research in constitutional diseases and working in the medical clinic at Johns Hopkins.

I accepted the job in Portland. The salary was to be $100, double what I had been earning. Withdrawing my last $100 from my savings, I bought a train ticket to Portland, but I decided to stop over in Baltimore to investigate the position at Johns Hopkins.

I arrived in Baltimore early in the morning and went out to my interview at Hopkins. After the interview they told me they would let me know within the next two or three days whether they could use me.

"Oh, please," I begged, "I have a 4:00 train this afternoon to Portland, and I must know before then if I am going to get this job or if I'm going on to Maine."

"Well, call us about 3:00 this afternoon. We'll try to come to a decision by then."

When I called at 3:00 o'clock, they said,

"All right, we'll take you, and you can start work tomorrow." I cashed in my ticket, got a room at the YWCA, and reported to work the next day.

My job was as a research assistant to Dr. Raymond Pearl. I still didn't like the city of Baltimore, but became very interested in what was going on at Hopkins. I made some good friends and met some of the best doctors in the world, including Dr. Ben Rutledge of Charleston, S.C; Dr. Baer, in orthopedics; Dr. Tom Turner of Prince Frederick, Maryland, who later became Dean of Johns Hopkins Medical School; and Dr. Baetjer, who was in charge of the x-ray department. Dr. Baetjer had been so often exposed to radiation that he had several missing fingers, but he was able to diagnose a patient even before reading his history just by looking at the x-rays. Also I met Dr. Helen Taussig who discovered how to keep a patient oxygenated during open heart surgery, and who started the blue baby project at Hopkins. (Years later, I had a patient,

Helen Wilson, about whom I consulted Dr. Taussig. The child was scheduled to be the first blue baby to have corrective surgery. Unfortunately, her condition worsened before the operation could take place. I was disappointed personally, because the child's parents were cousins of John Wilson, my first husband; and professionally, because I did not witness the first blue baby operation. Still later, I saw something in a newspaper about Dr. Taussig, clipped it, and sent it off to her. She wrote me a note of thanks, and the next week she was killed in an automobile accident.)

I boarded with two other girls in Baltimore. Johns Hopkins kept a list of boarding houses where students or workers at Hopkins were welcome. These boarding houses were usually private homes where one got breakfast and dinner with the rental of the room. A girl who worked in the same department with me shared my room during the autumn at Mrs. Ruggemer's on Guilford Avenue. Then, when I went home for Christmas, I learned that Katharine Moore would be coming to Baltimore. My Uncle Keene had found her a job as a chemist at at the Emerson Drug Company. She became my second roommate at Mrs. Ruggemer's.

Mrs. Ruggemer's food soon deteriorated from not so good to pretty bad. After we were served a meal consisting of oyster stew made with water, we decided that we would have to find our own apartment. Without too much trouble we found a small place on the corner of Mt. Royal and Charles Streets. Friends from Augusta gave us some kitchen implements, and we bought some cots. The neighborhood wasn't very good even at that time, because it was right near Mt. Royal Station. The steam engines put out a lot of cinders and soot, and our windows were usually open to catch the breeze, so sometimes our apartment became rather gritty. We were located across town from Hopkins, so I took the streetcar downtown and changed to another line. We two reported to Hopkins at 9:00 in the morning, but Katharine had to be at her job at 8:00. Since Katharine liked to sit up at night, it was always difficult for her to get out of bed so early in the morning.

As interested as I was in everything going on at Johns Hopkins, I still hated living in the city, so I often escaped to visit an aunt and uncle, the Bowie's, who lived in Upper Marlboro. One weekend in 1929, my aunt told me that Dr. Arthur Shipley, Chief Surgeon at University Hospital in Baltimore, had been tasked with finding a doctor to assume the practice of the recently deceased Dr. Russell Talbot of Dunkirk. Dr. Shipley, who was known as "King Arthur" in some circles, had a good many patients who came from southern Maryland because seriously ill patients or those needing surgery had to go to Baltimore hospitals. There was no real hospital and almost no surgery performed in Annapolis.

"Why don't you apply for the job, Emily?" my uncle joked.

"I'm certainly going to look into it," I declared, and I wasn't joking, at all. My aunt knew Mrs. Shipley from some of her club meetings, and I asked her to write Dr. Shipley requesting an appointment for me to meet with him in Baltimore.

In the meantime, a friend who had heard of my intentions said, "My sister, Mrs. William Hall from the St. James area, is going to be in town for the weekend. Come out this evening, and we'll introduce you to her."

So Katharine and I dressed up in our nice dresses and pumps, and we went out Charles Street to meet Mrs. Hall. She was really one of the most delightful people I ever knew! We talked about the country, and after some conversation, she declared, "Now, you realize that you just can't come down to the country in shoes like that!" Mrs. Hall was very down to earth and practically ran the neighborhood, telling everybody what to do and what not to do. After we discussed my plans, she said, "Well, I'll go home and talk to my son, William and ask him whether he thinks it is a good idea for you to come down to the country."

On the day of my appointment with Dr. Shipley, and with my aunt's letter in hand, I went to University Hospital. When I arrived, Dr. Shipley was in the operating room, but he had left word that he would speak with me between operations. I waited for him to come out, and when he did, he was a little intimidating. He was at least 6 feet 4 inches tall, wearing operating clothes and a green hat on top of his head. Dr. Shipley looked down at me over his half glasses without expression, then read my aunt's letter.

"Tell me about yourself." he ordered, after he finished reading.

I explained that I had wanted to be a country doctor since the age of 13, and I gave him a synopsis of my medical education and experience. I revealed that, although I was working at Johns Hopkins, I could hardly contain my excitement at learning about the need for a doctor in southern Anne Arundel County.

After he listened for a while, he nodded his head and said, "Well, if you really want to go down to talk to the people there, I'll give you a couple of letters. You can go down and make your own plans, but I want to tell you that you've got three strikes against you. First, you're little and skinny; second, you're a woman, and nobody down there has ever seen a woman doctor; and third, you are a Catholic, which is anathema in that part of the world ... they are either good Methodists or good Episcopalians."

I answered, "That may all be true, but I'm tough."

Dr. Shipley wrote letters introducing me to Mrs. Perrie, the widow of Dr. Perrie, and to Mr. Luke Hutchins of Friendship, and handed them to me. "Good luck," he said, as we parted.

# THIRTEEN

Mr. Hutchins was a bachelor in his 70's whose family was quite influential in south county. He seemed to be rather disgusted when the doctor he expected proved to be a woman, but I finally convinced him that I actually was the doctor. Then Mr. Hutchins began to laugh. He had arranged for his brother-in-law, Mr. Welch, to meet the doctor at the general store and to drive him around the countryside to get at look at the area. Mr. and Mrs. Welch had agreed to put the doctor up for the night in their home. Mr. Hutchins thought that a woman doctor was going to be a good joke to play on the Welch's.

When Mr. Welch walked into the store, Mr. Hutchins introduced us. Then, with a twinkle in his eye, he said, "Miss Hammond is the new doctor. I want you to show her everything."

Mr. Welch looked like someone had hit him with a stick! He could hardly believe his eyes, and Mr. Hutchins was delighted with his joke.

Mr. Welch and I went outside and got into his car, and we started out. Mr. Welch just sat there and drove and drove, not saying a word. I tried several lines of conversation to no avail and was just about to give up, thinking, "I just don't know where to start with him," when the subject of horses or horseback riding came up; and that broke the ice, because, although Mr. Welch was the village undertaker, he also trained and showed horses. He began to tell me about the country and who lived where, and we stopped and visited with one of two of his neighbors, and he bought some tomato plants for his garden. It was a beautiful afternoon, and the honeysuckle and daisies were in bloom in the country lanes. It smelled wonderful after Baltimore!

When we returned to his house, we sat on the back steps and shelled some green peas he picked from the garden. Mrs. Welch fixed a nice dinner, and afterward I went up to my room. The house had no inside plumbing, but I had a pitcher and basin and a lamp, and everything looked neat and clean, and I climbed into the bed and went to sleep almost immediately. During the night I became restless, and something caused me to wake up. I was full of bedbugs!

After breakfast the next morning, we went back to the store where Mr. Hutchins tried to interest me in buying a house. I barely had enough money to pay a month or two of rent, and surely didn't have a nickle to put into a house. I wasn't even sure that I was going to return to south county to practice. I wondered if Mr.

43

Hutchins' attempt to sell me the house meant I had his acceptance as the new doctor.

I returned to Baltimore that afternoon, and my next step was to communicate with Mrs. Perrie to whom I had the second letter of introduction. She was the widow of Dr. Perrie who had died two years earlier. Living closer to Baltimore in the Episcopal neighborhood, and being a pillar of St. James Church, Mrs. Perrie was quite prominent.

She very kindly invited me down on a Saturday, and again I was taken on a drive. On Sunday morning, she said, "I would like to take you with me to St. James Church so you can meet some people."

It had turned into a rainy, chilly day, and I had taken only a thin, white summer dress. I felt completely underdressed for my appearance at St. James, because everyone was dressed up. I was introduced to all the "Powers That Be" in that area, including William Hall, whose mother I had previously met in Baltimore. By that time, William had decided that it might be all right for me to come to the country to practice. I teased him for many years about being my sponsor.

I had been hoping that Mrs. Perrie would take me as a boarder and let me have for my office the room that had been Dr. Perrie's office. When I spoke to her, she said, "Well, I'll have to let you know. I'll need to think about it."

After I made the decision to go down to the country on the first of July, I again contacted Mrs. Perrie about taking me to board. She told me,

"I just won't have the space because my children want to use that room as a recreation room."

However, I believe she thought I was a poor bet for success since I was female and not of the proper religion. Nobody who was Anybody went to Our Lady of Sorrows, the Catholic church!

Mrs. Perrie, however, did do me a favor by contacting Mrs. Marian Hall. No relative of Mrs. William Hall, Marian had a nice house and lived with her mother and her two sons, Dan Thomas and Henry MacPherson. She agreed to take me to board and, what's more, said that they had a summer kitchen at the back of the house which I could use as my office. I took a look at the kitchen and found it to be in pretty poor shape because it had not been used much; but Marian offered to put in a coal stove for me, and I quickly accepted her offer!

On my own I had found a place to board and a place to set up my practice. No one was sponsoring me, so the acceptance of any one person or group of persons was not of much consequence.

Again, I returned to Baltimore, my head full of plans.

# FOURTEEN

The first thing I did was contact Uncle Henry, who agreed to help me get started by lending me $1,000 for one year at 7% interest. His one condition was that I agree to plant absolutely nothing for the entire year. He was well acquainted with my love for gardening and was concerned that I might easily be diverted.

I then asked for and received a leave of absence from my job at Johns Hopkins beginning on the first of July. They agreed to hold my place until September, but Dr. Pearl thought I'd not stick it out even through the Summer. All my friends at Hopkins had a dim view of my plans, and they, too, were convinced I would soon return, because it was the depths of the Depression and money and jobs were hard to come by. They didn't think I could make it financially, because I had no sponsor.

I went down to Howard Street to Patterson's Auction House, where I ordered a roll-top desk and chair, a metal cot with a mattress, a bureau, one or two straight chairs, and a folding screen. At that time there was a freight line ... a single truck, really ... that ran once each week, carrying freight back and forth between Baltimore and Prince Frederick. The freight line had been running only a couple of years. Prior to that, freight was delivered by boat to Galesville or Shady Side. I was informed that the truck would take the items as far as the crossroads below St. James, but then my purchases would be put out on the ground. This was because all roads off Rt. 2 were unpaved and a sea of mud most of the time. Fortunately, Marian Hall was able to get her tenant farmer to haul my furniture from the crossroads to the house with a pair of horses hitched to a wagon.

I bought a little car for $600 from Dorsey Gray, the head of the Ford Agency in Prince Frederick. Mr. Gray himself delivered it to me in Baltimore. He became a good friend, and I became very fond of Mr. Gray and his whole family.

In the meantime, I had no driver's license. I had been driving since I was eleven years old, and in South Carolina a driver's license wasn't required. I attempted to memorize the Maryland rules and regulations, but I was in a great hurry and hadn't committed the book to memory. When I went to the Motor Vehicle Department in Baltimore to get my license, I discovered that the man who was my examiner had come from Hampton, South Carolina. He helped me with the exam by asking questions such as, "Let's see. The lights are supposed to focus 250 feet ahead ... aren't they?"

45

"Yes," I answered; and with that very kind man asking me pointed questions, I passed the oral part of the exam. Then they took me downtown to Charles and Lexington Streets at 5:00 in the afternoon to test my driving. It was only a little hair-raising because of the traffic, but not a real problem, and I received my license.

The next thing was to get my medical license. Katharine Moore learned that the head of the Medical License Examining Board lived in Westminster, so we made an appointment and drove up in my little Ford. The examiner asked me some questions, and we discussed some things, but I didn't have to take a written examination, thank God! The examiner was more interested in where I wanted to practice and in knowing what kind of practice I was going to start. We talked for the better part of an hour. I like to believe that he wasn't harder on me because country doctors were very badly needed. I passed his scrutiny and received my medical license without any problem.

After purchasing some drugs and supplies to open my practice, I had just enough money left for two month's rent. One of the drugs I bought was a large jar of quinine to treat malaria. We had a lot of malaria in Beech Island, and so I knew something about it. I think I used that huge bottle of quinine only once, and then for a patient visiting from Memphis, Tennessee.

At the end of June on a day filled with excited anticipation, I loaded my car with my few things, and set off for Marian Hall's house in southern Anne Arundel County to begin my practice. We swept out the summer kitchen, and I arranged my office/living quarters. The cot I had purchased was used as my bed at night and as an examining table during office hours. The screen was placed in front of the bureau, and my roll top desk and chair were placed in the corner. I paid $50 per month for three meals and the rental of the summer kitchen. I then set the prices for my professional services: office visits were one dollar; home visits were two dollars; home deliveries were fifteen dollars.

Then, ready for my patients, I sat down and waited for an entire week without seeing a single one.

# FIFTEEN

*I think I was the first patient after the dog. ... It took people a while to catch on to the idea of a woman, and then she wasn't from around here, either. ... I just doted on her! I felt that when I went to her that she was going to make everything all right.*
Glorious Shenton

I would never have made it without Marian Hall and her two sons. They were wonderful because they acted as my guides during the first weeks of my new practice. Marian worked very hard to get them interested in me, to find ways for me to meet people and frequently drove me around to see some of the country. I tried to return all their favors in a variety of ways. For instance, Mac Hall was supposed to milk the family cows, but when he wanted a night off, I did his milking for him. Good thing I had milked cows as a child! Marian had a nice garden, and since my agreement with Uncle Henry said nothing about working in someone else's garden, I was able to indulge myself by working in hers.

One day Marian hurried out to the summer kitchen and said, "You must get dressed up because we have been invited to Mrs. Perrie's to a bridge party today. Hurry and change, and we'll go over to her house." I changed into a nice dress, and we were just ready to leave when a car came speeding up the drive.

"My first patient!" I exulted.

Several people got out of the car, and we saw that they were struggling to carry a large shepherd dog. After they got him inside, I could see that he had a large gash on his shoulder, and his owners proceeded to explain that the dog had been struck by a car. After I examined the dog to be sure there were no broken bones, I collected some supplies, and kneeling on the floor in my best clothes, I sewed up the dog's shoulder. When I finished, we put everything away, and then Marian and I went to play bridge. The people took the dog back home, where he chewed his stitches out, but recovered in spite of everything. That dog was my first patient after a week of waiting!

Then the Public Health Nurse requested me to look in on a young black girl who was dying of tuberculosis. There was not much that could be done for the poor little thing, except to give her something to make her comfortable, and I was saddened when she died a week or two later.

Tuberculosis was fairly common in the country. It is very contageous, of course. Besides the TB bacilli, it is caused by poor nutrition and poor living conditions generally. Patients were frequently sent to sanitariums, and doctors began surgical procedures in an attempt to rid the patient of the disease. Tuberculosis usually began in the upper lobe of the lung, and the surgeon would just go in and remove the lobe. It was the only treatment at that time, and it did arrest the TB, but one danger was that the patient might succumb to a secondary infection. This treatment was rather radical, and the patient was either a little bit or quite a lot handicapped, depending on how much of the lung was removed.

Gradually, patients began to come. At first there was a trickle, and then it became a stream. Of course, people didn't really have much choice. Dr. Talbot had had a large practice, and he had covered part of Calvert County as well as this part of Anne Arundel County. Annapolis was some distance, and there were no paramedics, no ambulances, and no transportation, except for that occasional bus that ran back and forth to Baltimore. Mrs. Talbot gave me a list of some of the doctor's best patients along with advice as to which of them would be likely to pay their bills and which wouldn't. She gave me a lot of things from his office, including a bag of dental tools which Dr. Talbot had used when the need arose, but I refused them, saying,

"You don't need to give these to me. I'm not about to start pulling teeth!"

I found, however, that the lack of dentistry was very important, because so many of the black people had terrible teeth, and often it affected their general health. Later on, health centers were developed for the indigent. The condition of the teeth of children and of pregnant mothers were of great concern. It was nearly impossible to find a white dentist who would see black patients, and even to get an abcessed tooth pulled was quite difficult. There was one white dentist, an alcoholic, who had an office in Wayson's Corner. No matter whom you sent to him, he would pull a tooth even if it didn't need pulling.

There were only two doctors anywhere in the area when I arrived: Dr. Cawood and Dr. Dent. In August or early September 1929, shortly after I arrived, Dr. Cawood became quite sick. He lived and practiced in Owensville, and was a very much beloved doctor. When he became ill, I examined him and tried to do what I could for him. Frequently, his wife sent patients to me because of his illness. I had to take over his practice, and this really caused my practice to burgeon. He lived about three years after I arrived, but for most of that time he was unable to practice.

Dr. Dent lived in Shady Side, but he was already in his 70's and not very well. He had prostate trouble and high blood pressure. He was a dear, sweet person, and a very good doctor. He had delivered most of the natives of Shady Side, Deale and Churchton. We

48

got to be great friends, and Dr. Dent helped me out of many tough spots when I needed a hand. He would laugh and say that he was always afraid he would meet me on the road because I drove like a bat out of Hell! I took care of him during his last illness, but we didn't know then what we know now about prostate surgery.

Patients began calling me for accident cases and home deliveries. Frequently, I had to have one of the Hall boys guide me to patients' homes. At times, I acted as a veterinarian, as well, because there were always horses that would get caught on barbed wire fences and gashes to be stitched up. After about two months, my economic status began to look better, and I was able to move to a room in Marian's house for an additional ten dollars per month.

In those days, most doctors didn't have facilities for an office, but had a small room in the house where they kept drugs and supplies. They didn't make a real attempt to hold office hours. Patients thought it was the doctor's duty to come and see them at their homes, rather than their going to see the doctor. I really tried to stress holding office hours at my office and made an effort to train people, but I was only marginally successful. Of course, I would also make rounds, going into patients' homes to follow up on treatment, and there were many home deliveries.

I wanted to apply for membership on the Staff of the hospital in Annapolis as soon as possible. At that time, it was a little cottage hospital, run by the Lady's Board. Dr. Borsuch was the Secretary of the Staff, and the Staff consisted of some doctors from Crownsville and from the Navy hospitals. There might not have been more than ten civilian doctors in the entire county. I went to one of the meetings and announced that I wanted to join the Staff, but, as usual, there was opposition because I am a woman. Dr. Borsuch made up all sorts of reasons why I could not be admitted. His last shot was,

"Oh, no. You live too far away so you can't be on the Staff."

I started to say, "Watch my smoke!" but, luckily, the rest of them decided he was wrong, and I was permitted to join. Shortly afterward I was elected Recording Secretary, a job nobody wanted, but which I was happy to accept just to get on the Staff. Even so, the Superintendant of Nurses and the head of the hospital were quite allergic to women doctors. They frequently made it difficult for me to get a patient bed in the hospital, protesting that they were overbooked. Sooner or later all that changed, and it finally got so I could function a little bit.

# SIXTEEN

*I thought I knew something about mud until I came to Maryland!*

Emily H. Wilson

In the autumn, the State began to improve the road in front of Marian's house. Their intention was to shape it up and put a layer of gravel on it. They got it all nicely worked up with heavy red clay, but then they walked away leaving it unfinished, and the rains set in! I got stuck in the mud nearly every time I tried to get in and out of the drive. We spent most of the winter arguing with the road people, asking them to repair the road at least well enough so that I could come and go in one direction. Marian even invited the engineer to lunch, but none of our blandishments brought a response.

Up the road from Marian's lived the Tillard Smith family. When Mr. Smith heard that I had arrived on the scene, he swore he would never let any woman doctor lay a hand on him! However, one night during my first winter, the family called me to say that Mr. Smith was sick with a very bad pain in his stomach, and they asked if I would come take a look at him.

I answered, "Well, I'll try, but I'm not sure I will be able to get there because of the road."

I got dressed and drove down the drive, and, of course, immediately got stuck at the entrance. I walked back to the house and telephoned the Smith family, telling them, "You will have to have someone come and get me."

They asked their hired man to get the truck and drive over to Marian's, but the truck promptly got stuck on the road. The hired man trudged back to the Smith's house, and got out the tractor. He was able to reach Marian's driving the tractor, and I climbed onto the back axle and clung onto the man's neck, while he held my medical bag in his lap. It was a novel manner of transportation, but I reached my patient.

I was sure from my examination that Tillard Smith had an acute appendix. He needed surgery, but there was no way in the world that we could get him out that night to the hospital, so I gave him a big shot of morphine hoping to stall the inflammatory process a bit, and we packed him in some ice. After this, I told him,

"I'll be back in the morning, and if you will send for me, we'll get you out and into the hospital for surgery."

"You aren't going anywhere!" he declared. "You are going to sit right here beside me all night."

So I stayed with him, and he had a bad night and so did I. In the morning we got a horse and buggy from a neighbor and got him out to the paved road and up to the hospital in Annapolis. It was fortunate that the appendix hadn't ruptured. He underwent an appendectomy by one of my surgeon friends, but he was very sick for about two weeks.

Thereafter I heard nothing more about a woman doctor from Tillard Smith. I took care of his entire family and delivered three more of their children.

From about the first of September until the first of May, I counted on being stuck in the mud at least once a day. I learned that there were certain roads that were passable only when they were frozen. As the Fall and Winter came on, the roads gradually got worse. I developed quite a reputation for knowing which roads one could travel in a given spell of weather. People would telephone me, asking,

"Do you think I can get through such and such road today?"

I'd answer, "Well, if you start early in the morning while the road is still frozen, you can get through there; but if you wait until it thaws, there is no way in the world you can make it."

There were only two paved roads in this end of the county, Rt. 2 and Rt. 408, and none of the private roads were paved, although the homeowners might have put oyster shells or poles in the worst places. Most of the patients I saw were at home, and often when the phone rang I'd hear,

"Our road is so bad we can't get out. Will you please come and see us?"

That meant that I had to get out of the car carrying my medical bag and walk about half a mile to get to the houses. If the call were a home delivery, I needed an even larger bag to contain the clean sheets and pads. Everything had to be lugged through the mud. Down in Shady Side the water in the ditches was sometimes over my knee boots, and there was no way to get into anybody's house unless you did walk.

People were absolutely wonderful about helping in those days. Often I had to find someone with a pair of horses to haul me out when I got stuck. I remember one dark night on Brooks Woods Road, I had to pull the car to the side because the road was too narrow to squeeze past the car coming toward me. As I pulled over, my car slid gently down the bank into the ditch. There was a big stump in front of me and another obstruction behind me, so I was unable to seesaw the car back and forth to get out.

The other car went on past me, and then stopped. Four men got out of the car and came toward me.

"Stay right there where you are. We'll fix it," they said. Those little cars were so light, they could just be picked up and moved. They caught the front end of the car and lifted it out onto the road, and then got the back end and lifted it out. "All right, you can go ahead," they said.

I never knew who those men were, but I can't imagine feeling safe in similar circumstances today.

I had one patient who was dying of tuberculosis. He lived quite a distance from the county road, so reaching him by car was impossible. I borrowed a horse and rode horseback to the house. I often rode horseback into the farms to deliver babies. It was a lot easier than walking because I could put the bag in front of the saddle. I borrowed a horse because I had no place to keep a horse of my own until after I was married, and sometimes I wasn't sure that even the horse could get through the mud. Many of the houses were back on the corners of the farms, and I had to walk across all the fields to reach them.

Redcliffe Plantation in 1989

Kathwood in 1989

Emily Hammond at Redcliffe, 1911

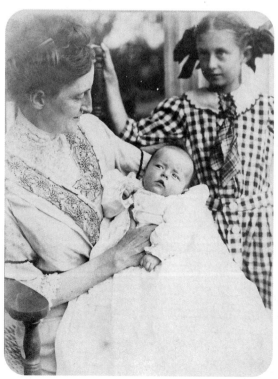

Mary Gwynn Hammond and Emily
Hammond with Keene in 1912

Emily Hammond in her
first communion veil

Pulling out of the mud at the ferry landing

Horseback at Kathwood

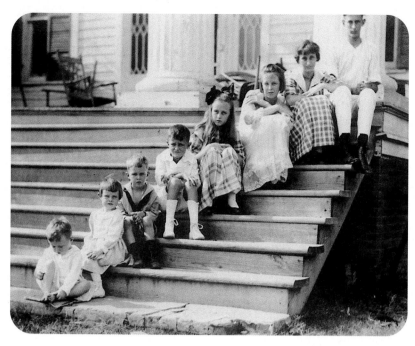

On the steps at Kathwood about 1920. Emily made the green
checked dress in the required sewing class at St. Genevieve's.
*left to right: Julian, Mary, Keene, Chris, Louise, Katharine, Emily, Harry*

Graduation from St. Genevieve's

Emily had to use old stockings to achieve this
hairstyle because she didn't have a "rat"

With the little horse named "C2"

Before the wedding, John and Emily drove to
Kathwood with Katharine Moore and William
Hall. Miss Nellie Hall despaired of Emily's little
car surviving the trip and decided the group should
borrow her car for the drive to South Carolina.

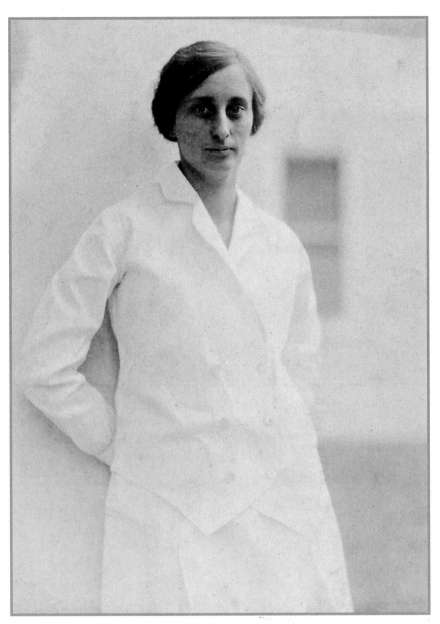

Wearing the medical uniform designed by her
mother at the Railroad Hospital in Savannah

Wide Hall at Redcliffe decorated for
Emily's wedding, 1932

Emily and John Fletcher Wilson
and son John, 1935

Emily H. Wilson with Chris
and John in 1937

Parents, brothers and sisters at Kathwood about
1936 with young John

Obligation about 1945

Crabbing from the dock at Rhode River cabin, 1947

Obligation about 1985

The dining room at Obligation
ready for Christmas dinner

The parlor at Obligation. Notice the
chimney cupboard

Entrance road in Spring

Peacock on South Lawn with "Red House" beyond

With Tup in Japan, 1978

You are cordially invited to a reception
to honor
Dr. Emily Wilson
for
50 years of medical practice in this community
three to six
Sunday, September thirtieth
Our Lady of Sorrows Parish Hall
West River, Maryland
surprise                    No Gifts Please

Aris T. Allen, Emily H. Wilson,
Virginia P. Clagett at the 50th
anniversary party

With Tup at a wedding in 1983

Emily Wilson with Bettie Wilson at a fundraiser in Pittsburgh

Christopher H. Wilson, Emily H. Wilson, John F. Wilson, Jr.

Emily Hammond Wilson and John Fletcher Wilson,
Emily's grandchildren

Emily Wilson on her 90th birthday, 1994

*Photo by Elena Shock*

With Muffie in the parlor, 1995

# SEVENTEEN

*...and there were so few Catholics! I had been raised with the idea of "Catholic Maryland." My mother had come from "Catholic Maryland."*

*Emily H. Wilson*

In the old days, there were at least four people, and sometimes six, on the same telephone line. Each person had a different ring ... one long and two shorts, or two longs and one short ... or some variation on the theme. The great entertainment was listening on the party line to everyone's calls. I was on the line with William Hall's mother, Nellie Hall, his aunt, and several other people. Miss Nellie Hall was quite a character. One terribly snowy night, my sister Mary answered the phone. While Mary attempted to learn some of the details about the medical problem, Miss Nellie was listening, as she always did. Pretty soon, Miss Nellie interrupted and protested to the caller,

"Now, you know perfectly well that Emily can't get out of that road tonight! Why don't you just take two aspirin and see if she can get out in the morning."

I had to explain to Miss Nellie that I was trying to build up my practice and would appreciate it if she didn't turn away any potential patients. Miss Nellie would give up listening in on the line for Lent; but it wasn't much of a "give-up," because she knew her sister was listening and would tell her all the gossip, anyway.

One of the other ladies on the party line was annoyed by the click that the telephone made when it was answered. Even if you didn't pick up your own phone, you could hear the clicking. This lady would take the receiver off and put it under her pillow when she went to bed, putting the entire line out for the night. She did this twice before I decided to complain to the telephone company. When the phone company repairmen went to her home the next morning, they found her phone off the hook and warned her that her service would be disconnected if she continued the practice.

The county sheriff lived just down the road from Marian Hall's house. His ring was two longs and a short, and mine was two shorts and a long. When I answered the phone in the night, still half asleep, the caller might ask, "Is Sheriff Prout in?" I was happy to say, "Thank God, no." I was always glad when I didn't have to get out in the middle of the night.

Individual neighborhoods were quite isolated from each other. People hardly knew each other in the same little area, and there was very little social exchange. It seemed that you knew one group or the other. Mostly it was just that people couldn't get around very easily. There was "The Swamp," which was where the oystermen and fishermen lived; and the farming neighborhoods; and the Lower Neighborhood, which belonged to St. James Church; and the Upper Neighborhood, which belonged to Christ Church in Owensville; and the Bristol Neighborhood. The Halls, Esteps, and Perries were the predominant families of St. James Church in the Lower Neighborhood. The Chestons and Murrays went to Christ Church in the Upper Neighborhood. People in the Lower Neighborhood joked that the Chestons spoke only to the Murrays, and the Murrays spoke only to God! Of course, people from Upper Marlboro in Prince George's County looked down upon all the unfortunates who lived in Anne Arundel County.

I started trying to get people together to become acquainted with each other. I began working through the Farm Bureau, and we had some farm management meetings. I had some friends in each of the various neighborhoods, and every now and then we had a party and invited members of the different groups at the same time. We achieved a certain amount of communication, but sometimes it was like oil and water. They all had pleasant backgrounds, but each group lived in its own little hemisphere.

Of course, in Prince George's and Charles Counties there were a great many Catholics, but there were only about ten Catholic families in this area. The whole neighborhood was very anti-Catholic. St. James Episcopal Church was the center of social life, as far as my group of friends was concerned, and it happened that most of my friends were Episcopalians or Methodists. Several times when I was in charge of church dinners at Our Lady of Sorrows, no one from St. James or the other churches came, except for a very few who felt sorry for me. I attended all the other churches' dinners, and I cared for their ministers free of charge just because they were men of the cloth.

Although I never would have become rich from my practice, I didn't seem to need much cash. I didn't need to buy anything. I didn't need any clothes. There was no great outlay of money, and I still had two months rent that was left over from the $1,000 that I had borrowed. Three meals a day were provided me, and because there weren't any restaurants in this end of the county, I didn't go out to eat. We played bridge and occasionally we paid a quarter on the corner for the bridge game. That was a great extravagance, but the bridge games were an introduction, and I played a lot of bridge.

Before the end of my first year of practice, I had repaid my uncle $700 of the amount I owed him, and he forgave the remainder.

# EIGHTEEN

For my first three years in south county, I practiced medicine in Marian Hall's summer kitchen. During this time I dated several of the available men and turned down two proposals of marriage. Tup would come up from time to time, but as time passed, I became more and more interested in John Fletcher Wilson. John was one of the stalwarts of St. James Church. His father had died at age fifty, leaving Mrs. Wilson, who before her marriage was Ella Gott, with five children and a mortgage on the farm. The other children had all left home, and John, who was employed in the Office of the State Comptroller, lived with his mother on the farm at Portland Manor.

John Wilson and William Hall were the two most eligible bachelors in the neighborhood, and I think that John saw a new girl in town and decided to date her ... and then he slipped! Someone complained, "John Wilson and William Hall were the cream of the crop, and the two new girls skimmed them off!" (Katharine Moore eventually married William Hall.)

I don't remember the first time I met John. He was a good friend of Marian and her husband, and was frequently invited to play bridge at her house, so our first meeting might have been over a deck of cards. Although John was nineteen years older than I, he was very young both in his mind and in his physical makeup, and we found that we enjoyed each other's company. We gradually settled into an understanding, but I don't remember when he proposed to me unless it was on one of his visits to Marian's house.

However, home deliveries interfered considerably with my bridge games and my party-going. I remember one rainy night John and I were at a party when I was called to Shady Side by a rather prominent family to deliver a baby. I had to leave the party; but John decided he wouldn't go along, so I got somebody to drive me down to the house and drop me off. John offered to pick me up when the party was over, or when I called him. The baby was a long time coming, but finally, I called John, saying,

"You can come and get me. The baby is here, and I'll be ready as soon as the party is over."

Well, I sat there and waited and waited and waited, and John didn't arrive. When I had given him directions to the house, I suggested that he come over a specific country road. It was a rainy, slippery night and his car slid over into the ditch! Of course, he was all dressed up in his best clothes, and he had to walk in the pouring rain to a house where he routed a nice black family out of their beds. They hitched up two horses and went to pull him out of the ditch. All this took quite a while, and by the time he got to where I was waiting, I was pretty hot. Not only had I missed the party, but I had been waiting a long time.

"Where in the world have you been?" I demanded.

"Where have I been? You told me to come through that road, and I have been in the ditch!" That event almost broke up our friendship.

Occasionally we went to the movies and to swimming parties down at Fairhaven. The first Christmas I was in Maryland, we went to a dance every night between Christmas and New Year's. In those days the dances were scattered all around the countryside ... in Laurel or Prince Frederick ... so it was always quite a drive. Once or twice we got home about daybreak, and since my office hours started about 8:00 in the morning, preparing to have office hours sometimes consisted only of changing my dress.

John and I were engaged for about four months before we were married in the Spring. But it was not all a smooth path.

My mother had come to visit me, and at the same time, Uncle Keene was in Upper Marlboro visiting my aunt. John and I made the mistake of going to speak to my uncle of our intention to be married, with my mother and my aunt present at the interview. What a ghastly mistake! In those days the Catholic Church was pretty harsh about requirements for pre-nuptial arrangements. John, whose ancestors went back to the founding of St. James, was a very devout Episcopalian and was on the St. James Vestry. My uncle, without any consideration for any of John's religious devotion, emphatically dictated the procedures John was required to follow if he and I were to be married. It was just too much for John to accept. Shaking his head, he said,

"I just can't sign those papers."

Sorrowfully, we decided to call off our wedding plans for the time being.

After a while, I had a note from his Mother in which she wrote, "I do hope you and John can work something out. I believe you two should be married."

Because John and I were very devoted to each other, we each thought that there must be some way to resolve our differences. We met for a serious discussion, during which I agreed to allow our children make their own decision about religion when they reached twelve or thirteen years of age. We got back together on that premise, but neither one of us really gave in completely. I wasn't about to join the Episcopal Church, and he wasn't about to join the Catholic Church; but we felt we could live together and tolerate each other's differences. He was very bitter about my uncle's uncompromising attitude, and he remained resentful of my mother throughout our marriage. She never realized just how much that session in Upper Marlboro had affected John. I don't think he visited Kathwood more than three times during our married life, and he rarely set foot in church with me.

On the other hand, John's family felt it was just as terrible for him to marry a Catholic. His brother-in-law, Guy Clagett, complained,

"I don't know what you see in that stringbean you're going to marry!"

I believe that he objected to my being a woman doctor as much as my being a Catholic. The Gotts were delightful people and eventually got over it, but John was very disappointed that none of them would agree to be his best man at our wedding.

At home in Beech Island we were a unit as a Catholic family, and I had been shielded from most anti-Catholic prejudice. When I married John, the opinion of our friends and families was split down the middle, but I felt no bitterness toward St. James or his people, even though they thought Catholics were a somewhat lower caste of human beings.

Attitudes have become less rigid now, but it was a terrible ordeal at the time, I'll tell you.

# NINETEEN

John wanted to have a big wedding. If the choice had been mine, we would have gone off somewhere with just the family. However, John said, "I have given so many wedding presents in my life, I want to get some of them back." That's the way it started. We got a tremendous number of gifts, and it took me nearly a year to write all the thank you notes because I was not very good about doing it.

We were going to be married in South Carolina, and Aunt Julia had agreed to allow us to have the wedding at Redcliffe. About two weeks before we were to leave, Dr. Cawood died, but I was able to get John's cousin to take over my practice while I was gone. I was particularly concerned about some of my older patients. I went to visit Olivia Lippett's father, Robert Murray, who had been one of Dr. Cawood's patients, and who was a very difficult patient in many respects.

"I am going to South Carolina to be married," I told him, "and I am going to turn my practice over to Dr. Compton Wilson while I am away."

Mr. Murray protested, "You just can't go down there and get married. I'm ill, and you can't leave!"

"The invitations are all out, and it's too late to change the plans," I said. Mr. Murray survived, and in fact, he and Dr. Compton Wilson got to be great buddies.

There were several parties before our wedding, both in Maryland and in South Carolina. My aunt, Mrs. Bowie over in Upper Marlboro, decided to give us a party before I went down South and had invited at least 100 people. John came to pick me up bringing a large box. I wondered, "Why would he bring me long-stemmed flowers to take to a party?" I opened the box after we arrived at the party and discovered it contained a bunch of carrots! Everybody had a good laugh at that. Incidentally, he also had brought along a corsage for me to wear.

Another party was given by the Chief of Medicine at the University Medical School in Augusta, and I felt quite honored by that.

Aunt Julia was a very cordial person, so for more than a week before the wedding, at any time she went to the store or saw somebody on the street, she would say,

"Now, we are having a barbecue on the day of the wedding, and y'all come on out to have barbecue." So in addition to the wedding festivities, she held a big barbecue at Redcliffe, and, added to the

100 people invited to the wedding ceremony, many of the people who came for barbecue simply stayed on to see the wedding.

My cousin, Henry Billings, was an artist, and he and his wife had arrived from New York for the wedding. He went out into the woods and cut down whole dogwood trees to decorate the wide hall at Redcliffe. Uncle Keene brought some elaborate church hangings, and an altar was constructed at one end of the hall. My brothers, Harry and Chris had rented tuxedos, but they had mixed up the suitcoats. Chris was square and not quite as tall, and Harry was tall and thin, so Chris' sleeves came over his hands, and Harry's sleeves were too short. I had to make them exchange coats just before the procession.

My wedding dress was one that had had been worn by my Grandmother Gwynn, my aunt, and my mother. Mother and my grandmother were both much larger people than I, but, even so, we couldn't make the dress meet around my waist because I was a different shape. I suppose it was because I hadn't worn laced corsets. We finally put a jabot of lace in the front and made the dress fit.

Joe Chaney from the neighborhood had agreed to be John's best man. My attendants were my sister, Louise, who was my maid of honor, my sisters Katharine and Mary, Katharine Moore, and another friend from college. They were dressed in antebellum-style dresses, and each dress was a different pastel shade of flower-sprigged muslin. My father, trying to be helpful, was wandering in the yard holding Katharine's dress on his arm, not knowing who it belonged to, or what in the world to do with it. Meanwhile, Katharine was frantically looking all over Redcliffe for her dress. It was very chaotic!

John and I were married at 6:00 in the afternoon in the wide hall at Redcliffe. A long dinner table for the bridal party was set up in the library of the house, and we hired an orchestra so everybody could dance after dinner. Although this was during Prohibition, somehow there was champagne for the toasts. A group of at least 20 people came down from Maryland with John, bringing some nice rye whisky which we used to spike the punch. When John and I left the guests were still dancing, and everyone stayed on for a long time. I don't know what time the party finally folded up.

Before the wedding, we had driven our car to Aiken to hide it from those who might decide to decorate it with paint and tin cans. Joe Chaney offered to drive us over to the hotel in Aiken on his way back to Maryland, and he had invited John's mother to return to Maryland in his car. She had bought a new hat for the wedding, but had left it in the car during the reception. When John and I left the reception with everybody throwing rice at us, we rushed to jump into the car. Mrs. Wilson jumped into the front seat and sat down on her best hat! She regretted that for a long time.

Joe was still wearing his tuxedo, but he didn't want to drive all the way to Maryland dressed in such finery, so when we arrived at the hotel in Aiken, Joe and John entered first so Joe could change his clothes. They spilled rice all over the lobby of the little country hotel, and by the time I went in, our newly-married state was no longer a secret.

Our honeymoon was a week spent driving back to Maryland, because I had to return to the office right away.

# TWENTY

*If farmers had a union and all the farmers joined, they could
run the world! But they are all such individualists ... I suppose
if they weren't, they wouldn't be farmers.*

*Emily H. Wilson*

After John and I were married, I moved out of my room in
Marian Hall's house and went to live with John and his mother at
their farm. Originally named Portland Manor, we called it Old
Place. It was a beautiful spot, and the property had been in John's
family for many generations. The original house had been built by
John's great-grandfather, but it had burned around the turn of the
century. Local carpenters had been hired to build the new house,
and that's probably the reason it was neither very well designed
nor very comfortable. Actually, it was a Victorian monstrosity!
Most of the lumber for the house had come from the trees on the
farm. The house consisted of a living room, dining room, kitchen,
and a big front hall and porch downstairs. Upstairs were five bedrooms, two of them quite small. They had added a summer
kitchen, which I turned into an office after I went there to live.
However, I found out before too long that it was impossible to
have an office at the house, because people still paid no attention
to office hours. We never knew if, when we arrived home at 12
midnight, there would be somebody sitting in the yard waiting for
us.

Mrs. Wilson was seventy years old when John and I were married. She was a very strong person with a very strong personality.
She was really quite remarkable, as she had for years raised her
family and supervised the farm, managing the crops, and raising
pigs, cattle, and chickens. There was quite a generation gap
between us, of course, but all in all, we got along extremely well.
However, the settlement of John's father's estate had never been
completed, so before we got married I told John, "We have to get
things settled." We had the farm appraised, and then held a friendly court suit. It was agreed that John and I would pay the other
Wilson heirs a certain amount yearly for their shares of the farm,
based on the appraisal. By doing it that way, we would become
sole owners, but it turned out to be a very strenuous undertaking.

We grew a big tobacco crop at Old Place, and, fortunately, we
had two very good tenants. John built a tenant house and a new
barn for the farm. There were 600 acres to the farm, and it was necessary to make them produce, but as always with farming, it was
very uncertain. John would plant with the idea that he would

make so much a pound for the tobacco crop, but when it came time to sell the tobacco, there always seemed to be a buyer's market.

We also had our own pigs and chickens and usually slaughtered one beef a year. We had a good vegetable garden and grew corn. There were several small grist mills around the countryside where the corn was ground into meal. We were pretty self-sufficient, but there were several small country stores, usually located near the post offices, where we could buy bread and canned milk and candy, and once or twice a week they might have beef or pork chops.

After the first year or two, we brought up a couple from South Carolina who worked on the place for seven or eight years. They lived in the small apartment over a new garage John built.

Of course, we lived on a road that was nearly half a mile long and up and down hill. You were more apt than not to be stuck getting in and out of that road. The other entrance or exit lay through four farm gates. Those gates were a great handicap when making house calls, because there were animals in the fields, and you had to get out of the car and drive through the gate, then get out of the car again and close the gate behind the car.

At least a couple of times a week if the weather was very bad, I had to walk the half mile from the house out to the road to be picked up by people who needed me. One thing that really used to irritate me was that, if it began to snow and it looked as though we were going to be snowbound, John would stay with somebody in Annapolis, because, weather or not, he had to be at work. I was left to my own devices to get in and out, and I had to pile on lots of warm clothes and go out alone in the middle of the night.

Down the hill from the house was a spring that we never quite conquered. A pool had been dug in the stream bed and an ice house had been built there in the early days. In the winter ice was cut from the pool and stored, covered with straw, in the ice house. It really worked remarkably well, and the ice would last all summer. Since there was no electricity, it provided the refrigeration for the house. Of course, it was also very inconvenient, because you had to carry the milk and cream back and forth to the ice house. Eventually, we got an ice box. We used chunks of ice from our ice house, or we had ice delivered from the large ice house in Galesville. We finally got a refrigerator run by bottled gas, and it was very satisfactory.

# TWENTY-ONE

Dr. Dent was really a very good old country doctor, but he decided that he had become too old to do any more obstetrics, so I was pressed into service. The doctor was rarely called to deliver a baby until the patient was in labor. There was no pre-natal care, and I never knew what conditions I might find when I reached the house, and it was unlikely that anything clean had been prepared. Sometimes I waited for twelve hours, or sometimes I would make three visits before the baby finally came. At that time, I was charging $15 for a home delivery, and if I had been able to collect all my charges for home deliveries, I guess I could have retired sooner!

The babies always seemed to come at the most inconvenient time and in the worst possible weather! One time they called me from Deale and told me that a baby was on the way. When I told them I couldn't possibly get out of the road, they said, "We will come to meet you at the paved road."

So, at one o'clock in the morning I walked out to the road by myself where I was met and taken to Deale. The baby was about to be born, and the mother was in a tiny room with a small portable kerosene stove. These stoves had no flue and no exterior vent. I had arranged a small contraption which held the chloroform-soaked cotton. The patient took a long breath of the chloroform when her pain started, and it helped a little. But suddenly all of us in the room began to notice that our eyes and noses were running, and I soon realized that the chloroform was mixing with the kerosene fumes from the stove. We had to remove the heater from the room, and when the baby was born the temperature was nearly zero. We grabbed the baby immediately and took it down to the warm kitchen.

I remember another icy morning when I got a call from the midwife down in Shady Side. She was a black midwife, and she was quite a gal. She asked, "Doctor, I wish you would come down. I have this young girl who has had a baby, and I can't get the afterbirth."

I hemmed and hawed and suggested a few things, but she said, "Well, I've tried all that, and I am just very worried about it. She seems sick."

So I got in the car. Everything was covered with a sheet of ice and the ditches were full of water all frozen over. I was absolutely sure I was going to end up in a ditch. The car skidded from one side of the road to the other, and, true to form, my front wheel slipped into the ditch. I had to stop and wait for somebody to come along to lift the car out. I finally reached Shady Side. In those days, the people had little houses, one room downstairs and one room upstairs, and that house was almost swinging in the wind. The only heat came from a stove down in the kitchen, and the upstairs room was bitterly cold.

The mother was a young girl, about fifteen, and she had already delivered the baby. It was quite small and appeared to be a little bit premature. I put my hand on her abdomen and exclaimed, "The problem isn't the afterbirth. She's got another baby!"

About that time, she began to have a convulsion. When I took her blood pressure we found it to be something terribly high, perhaps 200 over 120, and she had stopped having labor pains.

I thought, "This is it! I don't know what in the world I can do."

I determined that I had to give her something, a little petuitin, to restart labor, but I had no way of giving it to her. I didn't want to give her a sedative, because I wanted her to have the second baby. We had very few tranquilizers or sedatives available at that time.

She was having another hard convulsion, and in a panic, I called Dr. Dent.

I said, "Please come tell me what to do, because if I give the patient something to start her pains, she will go into convulsions, and if I don't give her anything, she's going to die because we can't get the baby."

After Dr. Dent arrived, he examined the patient, then he said, "Well, we can't get her to take anything by mouth because she is unconscious, so we'll dissolve some tablets of sodium bromide in some water and insert it in her rectum."

We used sodium bromide tablets as a mild sedative, and they were about the only thing we had. In this situation, it seemed to quiet the young mother, who again started into labor, and finally delivered the second baby and the afterbirth. I used this method many times afterward because it would usually do the job if you had a patient who couldn't swallow bromide pills.

Those twins were such tiny little babies! We took a cardboard box and lined it with a sheet, and then we put the two baby girls in the box surrounded by hot water bottles to keep them warm because of the intense cold. The mother had no milk, and in those days we didn't have formulas. I went up to the hospital and got mother's milk from some of the mothers in the ward. We fed those two little preemies on mother's milk at first, and eventually got them on cow's milk, and they survived.

Years later, a brother of the twins married one of Sam Pratt's daughters, and I was invited to the wedding and to the reception which was held at Sam's house. Sam Pratt was one of the very first babies I delivered in my practice, and I was acquainted with all the relatives on both sides of his family. When I got to the house, Sam, who had become an experienced caterer acquainted with everybody, knew exactly what kind of drink I wanted. He rushed to the bar to fix my drink as I walked in the door, but in his haste, he put quinine water in my scotch. But I got it down.

Near the twins' house, lived a woman who had had six or seven babies before I came into the picture. I was called to deliver yet another baby after she had gone into labor, and, because this was nothing new for the mother, I was sure that she would have this one in a great rush. My brother Julian went with me on this occasion, and we sat there a good part of the day. Finally, the baby did arrive, and afterward, the mother promised very faithfully and thoroughly that this would be the last baby she would ever have ... ever, ever! I think she finally had nearly twenty children; I've forgotten exactly how many. This couple certainly populated the community!

As I mentioned, we didn't have formulas in those days. We used cow's milk and hoped it wouldn't make the babies sick. When I first began to practice, Eagle Brand milk was a standby for all the babies. It was diluted with water, but because it was so high in sugar, the babies developed terrible diarrhea. It was possible to lose one out of three infants that way. One little baby they brought to me with diarrhea weighed less than five pounds, although she was six or seven months old. At that time we were just beginning to get some intravenous fluids in bottles, so I went up to the hospital and brought some back. I gave it to her into her abdomen, because there were no veins that I could get into. It's remarkable what difference even a day or two of that treatment made, and when she began to tolerate food, I threw the Eagle Brand milk out of the window and put her on a formula. By that time, I had learned that acidophilous milk or buttermilk could be used as a formula. She grew up ... well, she's a grandmother now, and is quite a gal. Her name is Audrey Parks Wayson, and her father later became a tenant on our farm, so I saw her through all of her childhood. She was fifty years old when I stopped practicing.

Julian recalls the time when he was sent for the forceps from my office. We were on our way to a party, but I needed to look in on a mother in labor. I had to stay with the mother rather than attend the party, and her labor went on and on. I telephoned Julian to go to my office and look in the top drawer of my desk for the big pair of forceps. Naturally, just as he walked into the house with the forceps, the baby decided it was going to come! Fortunately, we didn't have to resort to forceps very often, and I think I did only two or three forceps deliveries in my entire career. It really was a traumatic experience and took a lot of strength.

We took a big step forward later on when the Health Department was organized. As a matter of fact, we became the experimental county for the School of Hygiene in Baltimore. They were experimenting with home deliveres and home nurse practitioners. We had a five year grant which provided nurses to make home visits and prepare the house, making sure that there were clean cloths to use and a supply of newspapers to make pads for the beds. They would then accompany the doctor on home deliveries, carrying the large bag containing clean sheets and other supplies. It was a big step forward.

# TWENTY-TWO

*She was really a most remarkable diagnostician...*
*Sally Whall*

One thing drilled into us in medical school was to learn to depend on clinical diagnosis: the history of the patient, what you could see and what you could feel. There weren't the various laboratory tests and x-rays that are available now. One of the nice things about my practice was knowing the families and the background of the people. Sometimes I was acquainted with three or four generations of the same family, and there were many ailments that seemed to be common to members of each family. Some were more likely to have respiratory problems, and some more likely to have ulcers. That sort of knowledge certainly helped, and one became aware of the conditions after making home visits to people in the communities.

The houses were quite primitive in those days. There was no inside plumbing. We boiled the water to sterilize the instruments, and we boiled the piece of tape we used to tie the umbilical cord. Fortunately, the people were immune to their own surroundings, so it was possible to do a great many things you couldn't do in the hospitals. The people had lived with their environment. As they say, "the dirt in your own house is clean dirt," as far as you are concerned.

I began my practice at the absolute bottom of the Depression, and a lot of the people paid me in-kind with oysters, or chickens or produce, because there was very little cash money. The oystermen had a bad time. They couldn't pay their bills when the Bay was frozen, but even when it thawed out, they were getting just $.50 a bushel for their oysters. Many times I was paid nothing, but I received just enough to keep going.

Even after my first three or four years of practice, there were a lot of people whom I hadn't yet met or hadn't even seen. Many of them were still wondering what this woman doctor was doing, and I was accepted by many people only out of necessity. For instance, one rather hoity-toity lady who had a black cook called me to say that her cook had fainted and she asked me to please come to see her. The cook had been one of my patients, so I agreed to make the call. I went to the house and the lady met me at the door, looked me up and down and declared,

"You know, you aren't as bad looking as I thought you'd be."

Pulmonary infections were very common in the winter months, and a great many people died of pneumonia. There were no antibiotics or dependable medications for people with pneumonia or other serious pulmonary infections. When one has pneumonia, there is congestion in the lungs. Because of the build-up of inflammation and fluid, a patient literally drowns in the serum of his own blood. Most people died of being smothered. That's the mechanism of it. It didn't help that nearly everybody smoked, and many people wore long, heavy, winter underclothes which they didn't often change. When they came indoors in the evening, they sat by a hot stove, becoming overheated before going into a cold bedroom to sleep.

I think I was the first doctor in the area to make regular use of oxygen therapy for pneumonia cases when I learned that I could rent an oxygen tank and tent. We had the big oxygen cylinders brought out from Baltimore or Washington. We tightened the tent around the head of the patient's bed, and it gave a lot of relief to those people who were very ill with pneumonia. I know it saved some lives. One problem was that a great many houses didn't have electricity, and we couldn't have oxygen in a room where there was an open fire or an oil lamp. Sometimes the rooms were really cold because there couldn't be any heat. I used a flashlight to examine the patient when I visited, because a kerosene lamp couldn't be brought near the tent, either. We counted the time, and usually, anywhere from the seventh to the tenth day the patient would reach a crisis. He either began to get a great deal better ... the temperature came down ... or he went out. An attempt could be made to affect the temperature by using ice caps and sponges, but the best therapy was to get a good fluid intake and as much oxygen into the lungs as possible. That's why the oxygen tents made such a difference.

Sometimes we doctors did more damage than good, it seemed. For instance, when a patient was treated for ulcers, he went to the hospital and was given a little milk or cream every half hour at first, and then every hour. Nowadays, we know that the last thing you want to do is to stimulate the stomach juices by giving food that often ... the less frequently, the better. The use of mustard plasters probably didn't do any good, and very often it blistered the skin, making the patient more uncomfortable than before. However, I used to make mustard plasters myself and put them on everybody. It made me feel that I was doing something for them. I never prescribed purgatives because I didn't believe in them, but they were another old remedy. I remember my grandfather used to prescribe Colomel pills which were pure mercury. Why our teeth didn't all fall out, I don't know.

I had become quite interested in the treatment of syphillis when I was at Johns Hopkins, because Dr. Tom Turner was doing some interesting research on it, and I knew him quite well. When I came down to the country, they were doing blood tests to make the diagnosis of syphillis, but none of the older doctors had done anything in the way of treatment except to give patients a little mercury ointment to rub under their arms. I was convinced that we needed to treat syphillis, and discussed the possibility with my friend, Dr. Janney. Dr. Janney, who lived up at St. Margaret's, became our first real Health Officer and later went to the Disease Control Center in Georgia.

He said, "If you are willing to donate your time to give the treatments, we can get this new drug we are using, neoarsophen. The Health Department will furnish you the medicine, the needles and syringes, because it must be given intravenously."

A large problem was that we had no Health Center down in this end of the county. I think the first center we had was the polling house in the 8th District in the far end of Anne Arundel County. It had no electricity, no running water, and no heat, but only some tables and chairs. We began the clinics there, and finally, through the generosity of one of my patients, Mrs. Flather, who owned Tulip Hill, we were offered a house in Owensville. The house was in very bad shape, but we intended to transform it into our Health Center and a Boy Scout Center. This house also had no water and no heat, but it did have primitive electric service. However, the man who sold it to us began to go around the neighborhood whispering that "all of these people with syphillis were coming on one afternoon a week to take treatments, and this would be very bad for the community, because these patients would give syphillis to everybody in the area." Of course, most of the patients we saw at the clinic were servants in the houses of these same people in the community. However, they got up a petition and determined that we'd have to leave, so we did. That house is now owned by Dr. Wirth, my partner of many years, and he has remodeled the place into a very attractive home.

Our intention was to give the syphillis patients enough of the medicine so that they would no longer be contageous. If we could do that, it would stop at least the spread of the disease. Patients had to have fifty doses to be cured completely, and at one time we had some fifty people coming at least once a week, on average. It was quite a hazard because if you got a drop of the mixture out of the vein, the patients got a very sore arm for a while, and then they wouldn't come back. There were a good many people who didn't have very good veins, our lighting was poor, and the clinic took place in the evening. Additionally, after administering a specific number of doses to each individual patient, we were required to do a spinal tap to determine if the patient had central nervous sys-

69

tem syphillis. We performed these spinal taps at the clinic, which was, again, a little difficult. We had to seat the patient in a chair to draw the spinal fluid. It was pretty hazardous, but we were lucky and never had any real mishaps. The discovery of penicillen made the syphillis clinics obsolete.

Later, health centers were established in nearly every community. Each community was required to build and equip a center. I gave treatments in three or four of the clinics, travelling from one to the other, depending on the day on which treatments were given in each health center. Finally we got a health center on the Deale-Churchton Road owned by the community. I don't remember giving syphillis treatments there, but rather health and prenatal clinics.

# TWENTY-THREE

I found myself pregnant nearly right away. I was 28 years old, and John was older still, and we thought that if I were going to have children, it was time. I was thrilled to be expecting the baby, but it was very strenuous because I had a lot of morning sickness. On one trip to see a patient I got violently sick and had to get out of the car and sit on the running board. I lost my meal, but I went on and saw the patient a little later.

I was beginning to be quite busy by that time. I suppose I was seeing 15 to 20 patients a day. Most of it was house calls or home deliveries. Then, too, people would drop by my office at the house at any time. They had little respect for office hours.

My baby was due in February, but I realized that I was having problems because I had so much trouble breathing, and I gained about 20 pounds in one two or three week interval. We didn't let the family in South Carolina know of my physical problems, because Mother had a bad case of the flu at the time. In my seventh month of pregnancy, I suddenly developed pre-eclampsia ... very high blood pressure ... and for 24 hours they were afraid that both the baby and I were going to die. In those days they didn't know how to control edema and blood pressure, and they put me on a milk diet, which was all wrong. I had been taking soda to keep my heartburn down, and I think that was the reason I had so much edema. A lot of what was being done was wrong, unfortunately.

I was waiting for a doctor, a *locum tenens*, to take over my practice while I was incapacitated, but he continually delayed his arrival. He had agreed to come before Thanksgiving, but didn't get there until after the middle of December. The arrangement with Dr. Schulman was that he would take care of my patients until I was ready to return to my practice, at which time he would return to Baltimore. He lived in our house, had a guaranteed income, had free board, and he had the use of one of the automobiles. John and I each had a car, which made us a two-car family earlier than most, but the transportation was necessary to our livelihood.

The first morning Dr. Schulman arrived, he took my blood pressure. It was nearly 200! I had never had such high blood pressure before. He called my obstetrician, who ordered, "Get yourself up here to the hospital!" But I had to attend a home delivery before I could go. There were about six inches of snow on the ground, and the hired man drove me. When I got home, my feet were so swollen I had a hard time getting my boots off.

We went up to Baltimore to University Hospital where they kept me three or four days, hoping that I would go into labor and have a normal delivery. It was during the Christmas holidays, late December, and it was a terribly snowy, stormy holiday. John had quite a time trying to get back and forth to the hospital. I wanted him there with me, but it was difficult commuting between home, office and hospital.

I was given veratrin, which is a muscle relaxant, and shortly after I swallowed it, I began to feel like I was floating. The nurse came in and found that my blood pressure had dropped from something over 200 to just over 100. She became so frightened that they got busy and decided to do a C-section.

Of course, I was particularly thrilled when the baby turned out to be a boy, because John had wanted a boy. The baby, named John Fletcher Wilson, Jr., was very lethargic when he was born. The doctors said if they had waited another day or two, he probably wouldn't have lived. It was heartwrenching to leave him in an incubator in the hospital for almost six weeks ... nearly till the first of February ... before we brought him home. When I was packing to come home from the hospital, I found a mouth gag that they had prepared because they thought I might convulse at any time. I wasn't allowed to ride in a car or go up and down stairs or do anything for a month after I got home.

But the problem was with the baby. He simply didn't gain weight.

I didn't have any milk because they had put me on a diet and laxatives to decrease the fluid I had accumulated. My pediatrician hadn't been able to find a formula that agreed with him. For a week or two my special nurse would go around at night and collect breast milk from new mothers on the ward. It was the only thing that seemed to agree with him.

Again, I was very lucky. The doctor who had been head of Pediatrics at the University of Pennsylvania Medical College had just retired and had come down to live in our neighborhood. John finally persuaded him to come up to University Hospital and consult with the doctors. He was able to import from Pennsylvania a lactose formula that the baby tolerated, and John slowly began to gain weight; but it seemed to be a matter of gaining an ounce and losing an ounce.

One wonderful thing Katharine Moore (Hall) did for me at that time was to visit the hospital every day. Her office was near the hospital, and during her lunch hour she checked the baby's weight, keeping me informed of his progress. Katharine also stood in my sister's place when we had John christened in the hospital. I had asked a nurse to inquire if a priest could come to baptize John before we went home. The priest replied,

"He's had conditional baptism already because the nurse wasn't sure the baby was going to live."

I said, "I want him formally baptized."

John offered, "I can get an Episcopal minister, if you aren't able to get a priest."

However, I asked John to call Bennett Darnall, our friend from Our Lady of Sorrows, to see if he could bring any pressure to bear on the archdiocese. The priest came, reluctantly, and I've never seen anybody act so ugly! He pulled the cover off the baby, poured the water, said the words, and left. His actions only reinforced John's feelings about the Catholic Church.

The first night we brought the baby home we were as anxious as any other new parents. He had to be fed every two hours because he could take only about half an ounce of formula at a time. It was a 24 hour job, and I certainly was preoccupied with that for a week or two. It was worrisome for all of us. I was determined that John wasn't going to die, and, finally, he did begin to gain weight. It was in the middle of winter, and we were very worried about the temperature, and I am sure we kept him too warm at times. I had spent a lot of my medical practice undressing babies who had heat rash because they were too hot.

One month after I got home, I took up my practice again, because competition reared its head.

Just about the time we got John straightened out, Dr. Schulman came to me and told me that he was going to open an office in the neighborhood and he would be glad to take care of any of my patients.

"Well, thank you very much, but I will take over my practice next week for myself!" I said.

I was so irritated with him that I think it gave me the incentive to get back to work. John was doing better, and we had some help. We had a cook and caretaker, and from time to time, a daily nurse. I wasn't yet allowed to drive, so the hired man drove me, or the patients' families would come and get me.

This decision of the *locum tenens* was, of course, against all laws of protocol and ethics, because he was hired to take over only while I was incapacitated. One of the reasons I got him to come in the first place was because of an old lady and her brother who lived on Ivy Neck. They each had a heart condition, and they had fixed up a little office for him. They decided that since he was nearer to them, they would stay as patients of Dr. Schulman. He lasted from February to the first of September, when he realized that country practice wasn't that profitable, and he went back to Baltimore. Some of my best patients went over to him, although nearly all eventually came back to me.

Many years later, the niece of the Ivy Neck family continued to go to Baltimore to see a friend of Dr. Schulman's. After she had become bed-ridden, she called me and asked, "Would you please come to see me?" At that point, whatever satisfaction I might have felt didn't matter, because she was a helpless old lady in bed, and I took care of her until she died.

I had my so-called revenge a good many years later. I was in Annapolis at the Health Department to see Dr. French about some supplies. When I got on the elevator, there was Dr. Schulman arriving for a meeting with Dr. French. I went in to see Dr. French first while Schulman waited in the waiting room. Dr. French said,

"That man in the waiting room wants to be my assistant. He says he has been down here before. I thought you might know him."

I said, "Yes, I know him quite well, and if you give him the job, I will go on strike!"

Schulman didn't get the job.

# TWENTY-FOUR

Finally, John was retaining formula and slowly, very slowly, gaining weight. He didn't weigh six pounds until he was four months old. Like all new mothers, I rushed him to the doctor at every imagined symptom. Frequently it seemed that I would be running out of the house with the baby just as John arrived home from the office. Finally, John ordered,

"Stop right here! It is a piece of foolishness for you to be running to another doctor with the baby. You know what to do for him."

During one of John's vacations, we took the baby down to South Carolina for a week or so. By that time he weighed about seven pounds, and I was quite proud of the way he looked. Mother said later that she'd never seen anything as sad and forlorn as this little baby I'd brought down there! Returning from South Carolina in our old Ford, we had almost reached the outskirts of Washington when the baby began to scream and carry on, and we realized he must be hungry. We carried his bottles and his formula packed in ice, but in those days you believed the baby's formula had to be warm when you fed it. We stopped the car on the side of the road and drew some of the water out of the radiator to heat the bottle. I knew how to drain the radiator, because we did that in the old days during cold spells. I used to be a fairly good mechanic.

John's mother was willing to do anything she could to help. She was a very good cook, although we had a cook most of the time. She loved to spoil the children, and they were naturally drawn to her. For the first two or three years of his life, John frequently suffered with earaches and bronchitis, and had quite a hard time. Mrs. Wilson had a good many old fashioned ideas about medicine. One time John had been wheezing quite a bit before I left to go out on a call. When I returned, I found that Mrs. Wilson had decided that mutton tallow was the thing he needed, so she had rubbed his chest with mutton tallow and put a red flannel cloth on him.

I got a little mad at Mrs. Wilson, I guess, because I assumed that most of the furniture at Old Place belonged to the house. One or two of her children had taken several pieces when they were married. However, there had never been any real inventory or arrangement as to what furniture belonged to whom. When I was married, Mrs. Wilson said, "Now everything here belongs to you and John," but then this piece of furniture would disappear, and that piece would be given to John's sister, and another piece to his niece, or someone else. It was disconcerting, to say the least.

Every now and then I found time to swim or go riding. I bought a beautiful little mare at auction without realizing that she hadn't been thoroughly trained. She had a lot of peculiarities and was very frisky. Once she was roaming and playing in the field, and she rushed straight to the gate not seeing the bars until she was right upon it. She had to jump the gate unexpectedly, which spooked her even more. She never *ever* wanted to cross a bridge. There was a little stream at the bottom of the field where I rode, and one day it took me half an hour to get her across. I finally had to take her down the bank and through the stream instead of across the bridge.

When I got very weary and tired, and my schedule permitted, I would sometimes go over to Emil's on Connecticut Avenue in Washington. They offered a combination of hairdressing, mani-cures, massage, and other services. I spent about two hours having a massage and a steam bath, just escaping from the pressure. My sister, Louise, was a secretary in an international insurance com-pany and had an apartment on 16th street. On a weekend when I could get away for a while, I would first go to Emil's and then visit Louise. Dorothy Smith, Georgie Doherty's, sister worked at Emil's for many years in the hairdressing department until she opened her own little shop in Galesville.

At one time, John became quite interested in the prospect of having a good field dog. We got a beautiful Irish Setter puppy which we named Nancy. She was very affectionate, and we all loved her. People who knew about such things thought she had real possibilities of being a good field dog, and John took her to quite a few field trials. At one competition Nancy won a plated cup while still a puppy. We sent her away to be trained, but the trainer allowed her to be bred. Instead of being a field champion, Nancy was a mother, and became a family pet after the birth of her babies. We sold the puppies as soon as we could, except for one. This puppy was of a completely different temperament from Nancy. She was snappy and not at all the sweet gentle dog that Nancy had been, and we weren't as fond of her. The puppy was dognapped just before hunting season, and when she came in heat the dog-nappers let her get pregnant and then discarded her on the side of the road. They must have decided not to bother with her since she was not only pregnant but untrained too. Somebody happened to see her, and we got her back.

John and I were still playing quite a lot of bridge. John loved to play bridge, and it was one of the things we could do together. We had a group we called the Who Dealt Bridge Club. It was made up partly of neighborhood folks and partly of Prince George's County folks. We had dinner then played bridge, but sometimes it was dif-ficult to know whether there was a foursome for each table. One woman never let us know ahead of time whether she was coming alone or whether she was going to bring three more people.

Whenever we didn't have a nurse or someone with whom to leave young John, I took him with me on house calls. He was very shy, and when I tried to introduce him to anyone he was very reticent. I didn't allow John to enter the patient's house, except once or twice when I did take him inside to expose him to mumps or measles with the thought that he might get a mild case. The only childhood disease he had of any consequence was a case of chicken pox, which he had even on the soles of his feet! John, and later Chris, spent many an hour in the car waiting for patients to be seen or babies to be born.

I got to know Shady Side well. Travel was by a narrow, paved road that had deep ditches on each side. Anytime I had to get off that strip of pavement, I had to walk, and it was all mud. It wasn't long before I developed the habit of asking a family member to stand outside at the gate with a lantern or flashlight when I was called at night. In Shady Side I treated the Niemans and the Heinrichs and the Thomases. Old Mrs. Linton was one of the dearest people! She was an avid gardener and worked in her garden until a short time before she died. Also I remember Mrs. Wilde, who was my patient. She picked out crab meat, and I always bought mine from her. Once or twice I was called in the middle of the night by the people of the Masonic group. I had to wander all around in the dark before I found it because the place was very hard to find.

Glorious Shenton was always a patient of mine. She was the daughter of Mr. and Mrs. Andrews who ran the hotel where there was a crowd of people during the summers. Mrs. Andrews always said, "Now when you are down here in the middle of the day, you just come by and have some lunch." I would have the most delicious three course meal, and they never let me pay for anything, because I "was invited." I knew Mr. Hazard when he was a house painter. He painted Holly Hill at one time. Of course, I knew Anna Hazard's family and took care of her mother and father and all the rest of them.

There was a very interesting family in Galesville. Mr. and Mrs. John Kolb had settled in the village, and they ran the store. (Mrs. Kolb was Mrs. Andrews' Aunt Caroline.) They were of German descent, but I don't know whether they were first or second generation German. Caroline Kolb raised all her children in a large apartment above the store. I understood that it was Mr. Kolb who required their children to sit around the kitchen table and do their homework when dinner and chores were finished. He sat there with them, helping where necessary, and many people believe that is one reason for the spectacular success their children achieved. By the time I knew Mrs. Kolb, she was an elderly person and her husband was dead. She had two daughters who were graduates of Johns Hopkins Nursing School, and each was in charge of one of the floors at Hopkins; she had a son who was a doctor; she had a son who was a vice president of USF&G; she had a son, John, who was a steamboat captain for a while, and later started the store at Harwood; she had another daughter who was principal of the school in Mayo for years; and the youngest son, Francis, ran the store in Galesville. Still another son was in the insurance business in Washington. I don't know how she did it all. She was very low key, very sweet, gentle and unassuming, and the dearest little lady you ever saw. I invited her here to my house once, and she walked around the yard and saw some of the white flowers called Star of Bethelehem, and when she heard the name, she asked to have some. I dug them up for her, even though we thought of them as weeds.

After she got sick, Mrs. Kolb was bedridden for quite a while. One daughter stayed at home to keep house, and the family cared for Mrs. Kolb at home. They had RN's, Hopkins graduates, around the clock with her. I'm sure that much of the time those nurses knew more than I did, but Mrs. Kolb insisted that I come to see her every day for a year or two. She knew me almost right up to the end of her life.

I took care of four generations of Kolbs. The younger John Kolb, his wife and two sons, Clarence and Hopkins; and Clarence's children, Donald and LaRue; and Hopkins' wife and their daughter, Ann. Donald's son, David, also a patient, works for Mr. Shepherd in the insurance business. Hopkins Kolb was Postmaster at Harwood for a great many years, and he and Clarence later ran the family store there. They really were a remarkable family!

After the younger John Kolb's wife died, he went courting Mrs. Ward from Owensville. The family was a little upset about it, but she was one of the finest women I ever had the chance to meet. After the death of Mr. Ward, and at my suggestion, she had taken an LPN course at the hospital. She received her cap and worked at the hospital for a time. When she and Mr. Kolb were married, the family was a bit hesitant at first; but when he became ill, Mrs. Kolb acted as his nurse and took such good care of him that the family was very grateful to her.

# TWENTY-FIVE

I never wanted to have an only child, but John was not at all enthusiastic about a second baby. After what we had been through with our first baby, he was frightened at the prospect; but I wanted another child, regardless of the difficulties. When I became pregnant the second time, however, my mother and sister demanded I come down to South Carolina two months before I was due to deliver so they could watch over me.

My South Carolina physician was a man I had known in medical school, Bill Thurmond. He was two years ahead of me in medical school, and the brother of Strom Thurmond. Bill was scared to death and didn't know why in the world I'd come down there to unload my troubles on him, but he was very nice about it, even though every time I went to see him my blood pressure went up.

This pregnancy was a little different from the first one. I was thoroughly lazy, not doing anything for two months, and the doctor checked me every week. The edema and high blood pressure didn't get such an early hold on me. The baby was due the middle of January, but when I had an appointment the day before New Year's Eve, Bill again found my blood pressure to be a little high. I was surprised when he ordered, "I want you in the hospital, and we are going to do a Caesarian tomorrow morning. I'm just not going to fiddle around any longer."

"Bill," I accused him, "I know why you want to do the Caesarian tomorrow morning. You're going to a big New Year's Eve party, and you're afraid I'll call you away in the middle of it!"

I called John, and he came down on the train the next morning. Christopher Hammond Wilson was born on December 31, 1936.

When I returned home to Maryland from South Carolina, I brought with me the daughter of Mother's cook. Mrs. Enlow had been my mother's cook and housekeeper for many years. Her daughter's name was Georgia May, and, although she was quite young ... sixteen or eighteen ... she was wonderful. She was crazy about Chris, and as he grew, she was able to get him to do things nobody else could.

We didn't have the same trouble with a *locum tenens* as we had the first time. Dr. Linhardt took my office hours one or two days a week, and I named some of the other doctors who might be willing to see some patients. Additionally, there was another young doctor down in Calvert County whose territory overlapped mine, so the patients were all taken care of.

John was four when Chris was born, and we soon learned that

they were entirely different personalities. Where John was shy, Chris was outgoing. As youngsters they never were very congenial and always fought about one thing or another. For a while they roomed together, but that proved disastrous. John was always very neat and tidy with his possessions, but there wasn't a mess big enough to bother Chris, and everything stayed where it landed. When Chris was in second or third grade, he would walk home through every mud puddle he could find, and his clothes often were in tatters from fighting at school. Once when John was playing with Gordon Smith at Old Place, they persuaded Chris that it would be fun to parachute out of the attic window. They gave him an umbrella and pushed him out! Fortunately for Chris, there were some bushes below.

Although they didn't have a name for it in those days, we later learned that Chris had dyslexia, and it was severe enough to handicap his reading. He had a bad time in school because of dyslexia and because he was full of the devil! Chris didn't like school at all, probably because there was too much regimentation to suit him. He must have attended seven or eight schools before he finished. The winter he was in first grade it was quite hectic up here, so Mother took him to Kathwood and taught both Chris and Katharine's daughter using the Calvert School program. Mother taught them well, and Chris probably learned more that year than he did for the next several.

About the time we moved up to Davidsonville, Chris began to refuse to go to school, pretending to be sick. Then just as soon as I'd leave for the office, he'd get out of bed and go outdoors. Mother was visiting with us at the time, and Chris began to complain of a pain in his stomach. I had to get to the office, and Mother said, "Well, now, Chris, as long as you are feeling so bad today, you are going to stay in bed." Grandmother stayed by his bedside; and that totally frustrated him, because he hadn't had that kind of supervision.

Unfortunately, Chris was too much like me in temperament, so we clashed right heavily now and then; but Chris and his father were very close. The man who didn't want a second child became extremely fond of Chris, and they got along famously. Chris loved to help his father work in the vegetable garden. One day while they were working together in the garden, John sent Chris to the storage shed to get the fertilizer bucket. There wasn't much fertilizer in the bucket, so Chris opened another bag he saw there. He took the bucket out to his father, and they very carefully arranged the contents around the plants. Later they discovered that they had fertilized with cement!

# TWENTY-SIX

*Doctor did things no male doctor would do then or now. She was extremely busy. She had studied to be a doctor, and a doctor was what she was; people needed her, so once she got started there was no way for her to stop.*

                                        *Mattie C. Moreland, R.N.*

My life began to get quite hectic at the beginning of the 1940's. In the first place, nearly all doctors were called up to serve in World War II, leaving me the only doctor in this end of the county. The rationing of gasoline and tires was always a problem, since I needed available supplies of both to practice. None of my automobiles seemed to last too well because of the bad roads, and I had to buy a new one every two or three years.

I was entitled to buy tires if I really needed them, but otherwise the Ration Board was very particular about who got them. I was able to buy two new tires from the man down at the garage in Friendship. The tires he took off my car were pretty worn and only slightly better than nothing at all.

He said, "I don't want these. What do you want me to do with them?"

"Well," I said, "Just put them in the trunk in case I have a puncture on the road."

I taught a Red Cross Disaster course at the High School to a large group of people, and one night when I came out to get my car I found that somebody had broken into it. My flashlight and some other things were gone. I didn't realize it then but later discovered that the two old tires had been stolen from the trunk. I made the mistake of going to complain to the chief of the Ration Board, whom I knew quite well.

"What were you doing with those, anyway?" he countered. "You were supposed to have turned them in!"

I was in the dog house for a while.

Another problem was that I frequently ran out of gas coupons. Many of my patients would call, complaining, "I haven't got any gas and can't come to the office."

Since I was the only one who had gas coupons, I had a great deal of driving to do. The chief of the gasoline section of the Rationing Board was my patient, so I went to the Ration Board to ask for more coupons.

The man said "Oh, you're simply using too much gas, Doctor, and we can't give you any more until the first of the month."

"All right," I said. "but I hope you are the one who wakes up in the middle of the night with a bad pain."

"Oh, hell, Emily," he said. "How much do you want?"

During the First World War, health professionals learned a great deal about taking care of wounds, and some aspects of medicine advanced tremendously. After World War II, medicine jumped ahead again with the discovery of antibiotics. I remember that sulfa was the first antibiotic developed. We thought it was a miracle, and so it seemed at the time. People hadn't built up resistance to it, and no allergies were yet connected with it. It was given to anyone with a temperature, because doctors were sure it would cure any kind of infectious disease. Eventually, because of its extensive use, some people became allergic to it or the disease itself became resistant to it. Sometimes there were different strains of the same bacteria which didn't respond to treatment. Fortunately, about the time the problems with sulfa began, penicillin was developed, and then the myecins. Once they got in the "track," many new wonder drugs were developed.

There was also considerable progress in surgery, not that I was ever interested in surgery! What they can do now with surgical techniques and treatment for people of all ages is remarkable. I think the improvement in anesthesia was probably what promoted much of the advance in surgery. In the old days surgery was a terrific undertaking. Because of the long induction period encountered with the use of chloroform, the patient fought desperately for breath. Chloroform is, in itself, toxic, and can do a certain amount of damage to the lungs and throat. Often when I sent a patient to the hospital for surgery, I had to scrub and assist. I had to do a good deal of that. Dr. Wilkins once operated on one of my best friends for cancer of the breast. It was a radical, and I was the assistant, and I really didn't think I was going to survive the surgery! But you just do.

We were very busy during the first part of the war with Red Cross training, and we held rehearsals at Southern High School. The firemen come to the school to help because we had more than 100 people interested in learning emergency procedures. When they began the Fire Department in Shady Side, I was made an honorary member, and I taught Red Cross escape measures to all the volunteers, including the ambulance drivers, in Shady Side in addition to the classes at Southern High School. Many people were convinced that we were going to be bombed. A second evacuation center was located at the hospital, so we thought we were well-prepared. Our wartime precautions seem a bit naive now.

At the corner of Rts. 2 and 255 stood an old building which had been built during the First World War by Miss Eleanor Cheston, the sister of my friend, Clemence Burwell. A small encampment of soldiers had been located somewhere in the area, and she built this simple building where the men could come for tea and cookies. It had been rented to various people through the years, and when I first knew of it, a man and wife were living there. The building had no electricity or water and was essentially one large room, but, in spite of the conditions, I decided to rent the place for my office. We put in what was called a "sweat well," which was a shallow well only about 20 feet deep. We finally put in electricity, but we had only one ceiling light, so later we had to put in a few outlets. Casement windows let in so much cold air, that, although we had a good wood stove, it was almost impossible to keep the building warm. Eventually, we built a small addition onto the building. My waiting room was desegregated right from the beginning. This was somewhat unusual for the times, but it was the way I practiced.

My first secretary at the Tea House was Laura Hersey, who lived across the road. She had not had any medical secretarial training, but she became a very good secretary. During the summer of 1944, Sally Whall, Clemence Burwell's daughter, worked temporarily as my secretary. One day I was called away from the office by an emergency at Fendall Clagett's house. The Clagett's were my neighbors. Their first-born child, a daughter, had toppled into their swimming pool. They discovered her and removed her from the pool and tried to remove the water from her lungs. When the fire department emergency men arrived, they tried to revive her with oxygen, and, in the ambulance on the way to the hospital, I thought I detected the color returning to her face, but tragically, the child didn't live.

While I was away from the office that day, Sally mistakenly threw away a urine sample from a man who had traveled a great distance to leave it at the office, and took a patient's temperature after rinsing the thermometer in hot water. Both Sally and I had a terrible day.

It wasn't possible to see everybody during those busy years by making house calls, so I did a lot of persuading people to come to the office. I announced that unless a patient was desperately ill, he came to the office for treatment. Up to this time, I had not been very successful at training my patients, and many of them still wanted the doctor to come to them. Seeing patients in the office meant that I could give them better care because of having the proper equipment, such as the electrocardiogram machine and supplies of drugs for treatment, which I couldn't carry around with me. Of course, I also had a small office at the house, and after office hours, I made some house calls and also made rounds at the hospital. And there was always obstetrics! There was no way to control that, because it was a 24-hour-a-day proposition. By the time I moved into the Tea House office, we had about 2000 families on the patient list, and I was also seeing people in Annapolis and in Calvert County.

Mrs. Wilson had a good friend who lived near Lothian and who apparently had an endocrine imbalance. She was a manic depressive, and she would be fine for months at a time, but then when she'd revert to a manic state no one could handle her. She would have to go to Shepphard Pratt mental hospital for a while during those periods. I offered to drive her up to Baltimore for one of these sessions, and I was accompanied by Mrs. Wilson, who would, I hoped, keep the patient calm. Mrs. Wilson and her friend sat in the back seat of the car while I drove; and when we got to the grounds of the hospital, the patient declared,

"I'm not going in."

After some persuasion, she agreed to enter, but she bargained,

"I'll go in on one condition. You give me the papers, and I'll pretend to be the doctor. Then I'll go in."

So I decided that if that was the only way I could get her in the door, I'd humor her. I gave her the papers, and she strutted up to the desk, saying in a perfectly normal voice,

"I am Dr. Wilson. I have a patient for you.' Introducing me, she said, "This is Mrs. _____."

No one at that Sheppard Pratt knew any Dr. Wilson, so I tried to catch the attention of the admitting clerk by winking and making faces. Happily, Mrs. _____ began to exhibit the symptoms of her disease, or I might have been the one committed!

From time to time, John and I had been investigating the possibility of remodeling Old Place so that it could be made more comfortable. Eventually we became disillusioned about doing anything to the old house because it wasn't really worth spending any money on it. However, John had lived there all of his life and was very reluctant to move. From time to time I would find a likely place we might move to, but John quickly struck down my ideas, pointing out, "Now you know, Doc, there is no way in the world you can get in and out of that place in the winter." Building a road wasn't as easy as it is now. There were no bulldozers and earthmovers, and the roads were usually made with horse and drag.

Arthur Owens was willing to farm Old Place if we found a place to move. The tenants hadn't done a good job of growing tobacco, so Mr. Owens said he'd take over the place for the duration. I believe he was willing because there was a draft deferment for farm workers during the war. Mr. Owens, with his wife and little boy, moved into the big house at Old Place to run the farm. He was a good farmer, and, in fact, he later was named a "Farmer of the

Year."

We were looking for a house to buy and fix up, or for a piece of land where we could build. I looked at property along the shore, but even at that time, the shoreline was becoming rather well developed, and I wanted some space around me. One piece of property I investigated was where the Chewning house is now. We could have bought about 200 acres for very little, but we didn't have even "very little" at the time. The property was all grown up in briars, and I remember riding horseback to the top of the hill overlooking Herring Bay to take a look around. As early as Pearl Harbor Day, Louise and I went to take a look at Sudley House. At that time there was nobody living in it except a squatter, and it was in falling-down shape. I thought it was a very pretty house with nice lines and that I could do something with it, but that didn't work out either.

Finally, we moved to Davidsonville to a perfectly charming house which we rented for several years during World War II. The owner of the house was serving overseas in the war, and his wife decided to rent the house. It was constructed before 1700, but it appeared that a lot of time, money, and effort had been spent in fixing it up, and there wasn't much it needed. It was a telescope-style house and had a double living room with a fireplace at each end. John agreed to move to the house in Davidsonville, partly because it was half the distance to Annapolis, and partly because he was beginning to have health problems. We all liked the house very much, and we would have purchased it, but the owner wasn't willing to sell, and eventually, we had to look for something else.

# TWENTY-SEVEN

*Mother thoroughly enjoyed what she was doing. She didn't
mind stepping in where no woman had stepped before. She was
instrumental in knitting a close family ... and I've grown up
being very close to my Gott cousins in Pittsburgh.*

John F. Wilson, Jr.

Sometimes I wonder what would have happened to us if it
hadn't been for Estep Gott. As youngsters, he and his brother fre-
quently came down from Pittsburgh to spend summers with
John's mother, who took people to board to help family finances.
The Gotts grew up more like John's brothers than his cousins, and
John wrote a letter to Eas and Hayes Gott every single week of his
life. Eas was an engineer who had become Vice President of the
Dravo Company in Pittsburgh, and was considered the best tunnel
man in the United States. He had always wanted a place in the
Maryland countryside, but he was not yet ready to retire.

George Morris was a Scripps-Howard newspaperman who,
along with his wife Carrie, owned a property named Etowah located on Rt. 2. The Morrises had lived there for five or six years and
had fixed up the house. He had been a heart patient of mine, and
although we got him through his first heart attack, near the end of
the war he died of a second massive coronary. After George's
death, Carrie didn't want to live alone at Etowah, and decided to
put the property on the market. I spoke to Eas about the property,
and he proposed,

"I will buy it, if you and John will live in the house and keep the
farm going until I am ready to retire."

Since we had to leave the Davidsonville house, we accepted his
offer without delay. Eas realized that John's health was deteriorat-
ing, and for John it was a Godsend, because he had developed very
high blood pressure and our farm worried him to death.

Etowah was in good shape. It was heated and comfortable and
had been lived in and cared for. It looks like a city house in the
country, because it resembles a three story townhouse. Perhaps
that style was a fad during the early 1800's, because it is similar to
Roedown and Contee Place, two old Maryland homes. The original house is made of brick, with a newer frame wing containing a
kitchen, a den with fireplace, and a bedroom and bath upstairs,
along with a maid's bedroom and bath. I understood that Etowah
had belonged to Robert E. Lee's sister, and that two of his sisters
lived there at one time.

We had a delightful time living in that house, because it was rather like living in a condominium where you could call the landlord and say, "We need to have this or that repaired." Eas paid all the bills and didn't charge us anything because we compensated by supervising Mr. John Watkins (who lived there until recently). Eas was a benevolent landlord, thank goodness. However, one time when he came down to visit, he really raised a fuss! The tenant raised pigs, and the little pigs would get out into the yard even though we had asked the tenant to keep them penned up. Eas was a very meticulous person. He finally blew a fuse, storming,

"You just can't keep on letting them ruin the yard like this!"

Realizing that John Watkins got most of the share of the pigs, I warned him,

"If you let these pigs get into the yard again, we're going to catch one, and we're going to have roast pig!"

Mr. Watkins laughed about it then; but, sure enough, after we found the pigs again in the yard, we caught one, and we cooked roast pig. When Hope Andrews and Frances Kelly published "Maryland's Way," my friend, Stephanie Rich surprised me by entering a recipe for roast pig under my name.

The boys had a good time while we lived at Etowah. Rena Watkins, our cook, had 21 living children, so there were the makings of two softball teams right there.

Some of the nicest pieces of furniture I own were accumulated from various patients. In the early 1900's many people thought that golden oak was much more fashionable than walnut or mahogany, and some nice old pieces were discarded. Many of the pieces I found had been broken. For instance, a table that I still use came from a black family whose baby I delivered but who had no money to pay the bill. The table top was in two pieces and the legs were wrapped with wire to hold them together. I could see that the table had been a good piece originally, and when the family told me they couldn't pay me, I offered to cancel part of their bill in exchange for the table. I delivered babies in the bed I sleep in now; and at some point I had the roll top removed from my original auction house office desk, and I still use the desk.

Later on, I collected everything I could think of that was old, including millstones from peoples' yards. When the huge stones got to the point where they were not sharp enough to grind the meal, they were replaced. One of them I remember particularly. I offered to take the millstone instead of a fee, and the lady of the house said,

"You can't get it into that car, so you'll have to let us know how we can deliver it to you."

However, I learned fairly early in my life that if somebody was willing to sell me something or give it to me, I should accept it right then because there might never be another chance. So we got a plank and rolled the stone up into the back of the Ford. The car sank so far under its weight that I wasn't sure I'd get it home.

Life was pretty strenuous during these days. There was my practice, and John's health, and the tenant at Old Place, and the boys' education. We didn't have any money, but I had a good friend, Howard Atterbury, who was a patient, and who lived at Maidstone, St. Margaret's. He was a cousin of John's and a first cousin of the Gott's. Howard had some very good connections, and he was able to get a scholarship for John at the Hill School. At that time, Hill was attempting to broaden the background of its student body by finding students from families of more moderate means, into which category we certainly fit.

Because I worked once or twice a month at the Childrens' and Mothers' Clinics of the Health Department, many of the pregnant ladies knew me. One very cold night about 11:30 or 12:00, a car drove up blowing the horn, so I knew it was an emergency of some kind. We went down to the car, and found a woman who had delivered a baby on the back seat. She had started out for the hospital, but the baby was born before they reached Baltimore, so they turned around and drove into the yard. We got a blanket and wrapped the baby in it, and then cut the cord and delivered the afterbirth. While the couple went back home to fetch some baby clothes, we took the baby into the kitchen. Later, we dressed the baby, and I sent them all home. I don't think they ever got near the hospital.

The ambulance pulled that trick quite often. When ambulances began to be available, some of the black patients would call the ambulance to take them up to Johns Hopkins. Black people had to go to Hopkins to be delivered because the Annapolis hospital did not do black deliveries. Many patients would not be in true labor and were sent home, but many babies would arrive on the way to Baltimore. If the baby arrived before the ambulance crossed the South River Bridge, the ambulance turned around and came back, and I would finish up the job. This occurred routinely four or five times a week. When we finally bought Obligation, I didn't want our name at the entrance or anywhere near the place, but it didn't take people very long to find out where we lived.

I lost my Aunt Julia during these years. She had finally married when she was 50 years old, and she and her husband, James Richards, lived at Redcliffe. They had been married for 28 years, when, one day somebody threw a cigarette into the woods. Uncle Jim went down to help put out the fire, and when he returned to the house, he had a heart attack and died. Aunt Julia never recovered, and she became pathologically depressed. Her long illness became quite a problem for the family, and Mother went to Redcliffe to stay with her for a while before they hired a live-in nurse. They didn't tell me about Aunt Julia's death until it was too late for us to get to the funeral. In those days, there were very few airplanes, and John had a serious eye infection, so we couldn't drive.

All the Hammonds were buried the next day after death, if at all possible. My Grandfather Hammond was buried quickly because they were afraid to open his will until after he had been safely buried. He had threatened that he wanted to be buried standing up in a pine box. His will contained no such provision, but since he was such a character, no one could have been sure.

My Uncle Henry, the judge who lived in Augusta, also had his eccentricities. He insisted that his tailor line the back as well as the front of the vests matching his suits. Additionally, as the city encroached upon his property, he moved farther into the country-side. He did this several times, because he didn't want to live in town. At last, he owned about 30 acres, and he built a large two story house, quite grand, with all the required rooms and equip-ment, and with lovely gardens planted in camellias. However, Uncle Henry didn't build a staircase to the second floor because he didn't want guests. Instead, there was a ladder placed outside to an upstairs window. As I remember, the only person who had the courage to spend the night and take advantage of this hospitality was John Billings' brother, Henry, who had decorated Redcliffe's wide hall for my wedding.

Redcliffe was partly owned by Uncle Henry, but he cared noth-ing for the place. After Aunt Julia's death, Uncle Henry didn't want to move to Redcliffe and didn't want the responsibility of its maintenance. Aunt Julia's nephew, John Billings, who had a very successful career as managing editor of Time, Life and Fortune, bought Redcliffe for $1,500! He wasn't ready to retire, so the house remained largely uninhabited for at least fifteen years. Redcliffe eventually was given to the State of South Carolina and is now an historic site open to the public.

# TWENTY-EIGHT

In 1945 at the end of World War II, our first vacation was spent in Maine. My friend, Catrina Bowie, who lived in Bay Ridge and who owned much of that property, had grown up in Maine as a child. Her mother and father had gone cruising on their honeymoon, and the boat stopped for a few hours on Swan's Island. They liked it so much that they had a house built on a very beautiful spot on the island.

John and I drove up in our little Ford with my cousin, Louise Hall, and with Catrina's husband, Page Bowie. Catrina had gone ahead to Maine. As we packed for the trip, John instructed me not to take my medical bag because everybody on the island would soon learn about my being a doctor, and I would be unable to rest.

The night of our arrival John had a coronary! He suffered the most terrible pain all night, and I had nothing with me but phenobarbitol and aspirin. We were very lucky, because Catrina knew of a Dr. Clark from Washington who had a place at Southwest Harbor. I called him that night, using the only telephone on the island. He came the next morning by boat and brought what medicine he thought was necessary.

We had been invited to stay with Catrina in Maine for two weeks. Our visit was extended to six weeks, because John couldn't possibly travel. The doctor wouldn't let him get out of bed or do anything for himself. Maine was a wonderful place for John's recuperation. He had no worries, and it was quiet and cool. It became quite chilly before we left, but we really enjoyed it, because all the tourist commotion was over.

We asked to have a maid and a cook sent from Maryland to Maine to help us, and the maid brought my medical bag along. The island had no doctor, but there was a practical nurse. One of the mainland churches sent the nurse over by boat once a week to check on the islanders. After discovering that I was a doctor, the visiting nurse made a deal with me. She proposed,

"I will come and give John a massage and a bed bath, if you will make rounds with me and perform physicals on the pregnant ladies."

It really was quite interesting because I was able to meet some of the local people. Once in the middle of the night they asked me to help treat one of the islanders who was hemorrhaging from a stomach ulcer. The Red Cross boat, supplied with some emergency equipment (plasma and outfits for intravenous medicines), had arrived to look in on him; so I went to give him his IV's.

Young John had been at camp on Lake Winnepesaukee that summer where he was taking a refresher course which would permit him to skip from the seventh to the ninth grade when he entered Hill. We had planned to pick him up at camp and take him back to Etowah and get him ready to go to school; but I couldn't leave because of John's recuperation. Page Bowie picked him up and brought him to Swan's Island for a couple of days. The night he arrived we had lobsters for dinner. I believe John was thirteen at the time, and I doubt if he had ever before eaten a lobster. Fortunately, we had bought a few extra, because John ate not only one, but two big lobsters, and there started a lifelong passion! After a few days, we sent him back to Maryland to his grandmother and his great aunt so they could get him packed and sent to school.

While he was at Hill, John enjoyed frequent and informative letters from his father. However, he chides me that I wrote only a line or two about the snow or mud, enclosed a check, then signed the letter, "Love, Emily H. Wilson, M.D."

Chris, of course, was always a problem. We had a good cook who spoiled him, and he had more fun with Gladys Reed than he did with his family. He'd pull the choice meats from the freezer and ask Gladys to prepare them. After attending Hill School, which he hated with a passion, Chris went to St. Mary's in Annapolis. He started school in September, and he felt so much at home at St. Mary's that by late October he had been elected President of his class. However, his scholastic work left something to be desired.

Springtime really got to Chris, because he loved to be in the country. He and the president of the Student Council, Bill McWilliams, Jr., disappeared from St. Mary's one Spring day. The nun called me and asked,

"Where is Chris? We haven't seen him today. What has happened to him?"

I learned that he and Bill had driven down in Bill's car with two other boys and were here just enjoying the farm. Chris was nearly expelled for that escapade.

We returned to Swan's Island nearly every summer after that year because John had really come to love it. I think Swan's Island is the most beautiful spot I've seen anywhere. The people of the island were a sturdy lot, all in all, but every summer there was at least one emergency. I concentrated primarily on pre-natal care, and fortunately, the women were pretty healthy. We worked very hard to get emergency services organized for that coast, and eventually we were successful in obtaining some paramedics. However, there were two people who almost died in my hands on the island. I felt very helpless at those times.

One year the New York Cruising Club held a large sailboat race while we were there. The boats spent the night in the little harbor, and the next morning we all went out to the Point to watch them take off. There must have been several hundred boats, and I've never seen such beautiful spinnakers! After we returned to Catrina's cottage, to our great delight, the boats sailed directly in front of the house, almost within touching distance. We took our lunches out to the porch that day so as not to miss any of the parade.

Some years later, Catrina and I together bought a place on the island. Adjoining her property there were some ten acres which had probably been a small vegetable farm. This ten acres protected the privacy of Catrina's property because it lay between her house and the road. The former owner had been a lobsterman, and he'd owned the 3-story house and a large barn in which he had constructed his boat. The barn had been abandoned with all sorts of interesting junk in it, such as lots of old license plates and tools. I kept the property for several years.

# TWENTY-NINE

*I went in to help at the front desk ... and stayed for 18 years!*
*The Tea House was a very small place, and I remember it was*
*almost always cold. Doctor was a very fast worker, and we had*
*to be on our toes to stay one jump ahead of her.*

*Margie Moreland*


As far as I know, I diagnosed the first case of tick fever in
Maryland. We didn't have much of it on the East Coast. It was
commonly called Rocky Mountain Spotted Fever because it started out west. The disease was spread by cattle, and I suppose cattle
brought it into Maryland. Most of the infected ticks seemed to be
located around Shady Side and Churchton. Tick fever was one of
the most serious diseases we dealt with because the symptoms are
rather common to a number of diseases, making it difficult to diagnose. The distinctive mark of tick fever doesn't come until well
after the onset of the disease, and the blood test took so long in
those days that the patient had either recovered ... or "otherwise."

I was called to look at a child down in Churchton who had a
headache and high temperature. The family knew that this child
had been bitten by a tick, which was very helpful to the diagnosis.
Of course, a lot of people have been bitten by ticks, as have I; but,
because this child was very sick, I thought tick fever might be the
cause. He also had a rash on the palms of his hands and on the
soles of his feet which eventually spread over his body.

Several doctors from Johns Hopkins School of Medicine came to
see my patient to observe the symptoms, especially the rash which
gives the disease its name. Fortunately, this patient was a child,
because in people over 50 years of age, the mortality rate was
almost 75%. I had one or two patients who died of tick fever.
People became terribly ill for a while with a temperature of 105 or
106 degrees, along with headache. When patients started off that
way, the doctor was just prepared for the worst. We didn't have
much to give for the disease but fluids and something for the
headache pain ... ice caps and sponge baths to bring the temperature down. Prayer and Hope. In those days, we didn't have a drug
to treat it, but now some of the myecins are specific for Rocky
Mountain Spotted Fever, and if it is suspected, the patient is started on a drug immediately, even before a positive blood test is
achieved.

Although there were farm accidents that happened frequently, I
have never forgotten a particularly terrible one. It happened in the

93

Spring at tobacco planting time. When tobacco is planted, each plant is set into a hole along with some water. The water is carried to the fields in a large tank set on a carriage or trailer. Mrs. Frank Catterton had been working in the tobacco field, and, intending to take a break, she sat down on the tongue of the cart. The entire tank of water tipped and fell over on her, crushing her head. They rolled the tank away and called me. After I had walked out into the field and examined her, I knew there was little to be done. She was screaming in agony, and although I gave her enough morphine to put her out, it had no effect. I stayed with her in the field holding her hand until the ambulance came. All the way to the hospital and all the while she was in the hospital she screamed, but there was nothing anyone could do for her. She died a slow death, and her screams haunted me for a long time.

I was invited to be on the first Board of Anne Arundel Community College. We began by having our meetings at the Severna Park High School, and the Board appointed the first college President. Classes were held in the High School, and we enlisted some teachers from the Naval Academy who moonlighted as faculty for the new Community College. We discussed buying a piece of land on which to establish a campus, but while I was on the Board we got no farther than talking about it. The state was contemplating the construction of another north-south highway to the east of Ritchie Highway at the time, and the Board was cautious about purchasing any land. Eventually, the College Board did purchase property east of Ritchie Highway, and the new highway, Rt. 97, was built to its west instead.

# THIRTY

After Arthur Owens left the farm at Old Place, it fell to me to oversee most of the farming there, in addition to the responsibilities at Etowah. We suffered two rather incompetent tenants, who proceeded to take Old Place apart while living there. The tenants were also entrusted with the care of 30 purebred sheep. One morning at about 5:00 o'clock, one of the tenants called me exclaiming, "Come down and see! All the sheep are dead!"

I got dressed and went down alone. I didn't want to alarm John because he was still convalescing from his heart attack, and we hadn't been able to control his blood pressure. When I arrived at Old Place, I saw the sky filled with buzzards. I've never seen so many! The tenant and I began to walk across the field in back of the house seeing sheep carcasses in various stages of decomposition scattered all across the field. Apparently wild dogs had been coming for a period of a week or ten days to get at them. The tenant had been instructed to put the sheep in the barn every night, but had simply neglected to do so. I couldn't believe he didn't realize something was amiss when fewer and fewer sheep came to be fed each day!

We had been living at Etowah for three years, when one day Laura Hersey came to me and told me that the neighboring property, Obligation, had been put on the market. Laura was the niece of Mr. Bassford, who was the caretaker of the property. The warrant for Obligation is dated 1671, when King Charles II granted the property to Thomas Stockett in 'obligation' to Stockett for his service. The farm belonged to General Henry Warfield, Wallis Windsor's Uncle Henry. His wife was a Stockett, and the place had been in her family since 1671. General Warfield lived in Baltimore and hadn't seen the property for at least 20 years.

Although I could see that the house had real possibilities, I was quite hesitant about it, because the situation was grim. At first there had been decent tenants on the farm, but for the previous five years or so, squatters had taken over the place. These people had raised pigs and chickens in the den and had stripped tobacco in the parlors. On the third floor we found evidence of a still, and the odor of the mash permeated the upstairs. We found a pile of rags they'd used for a bed in a corner of a second floor room. There was no central heating, no plumbing, no water, and no electricity. The yard was fenced for pasture and had horses and cattle roaming through it. The outbuildings consisted of one tobacco barn, a stable, and a tiny and very old cornhouse.

There was absolutely no landscaping of any kind around the house, except for one large oak tree, because everything else had been burned for firewood. The box bushes were holes in the dirt from the cattle rubbing against them. Only ten acres of arable land had been worked in the previous five years, and all the other fields were overgrown with locust and pine scrub. The road was nearly impassible. From time to time when I took people to see the place, we were unable to drive over the deep cut road, but had to walk. That road was probably original to the property.

Laura's brother wanted to buy the entire 900 acres, but somehow she persuaded Mr. Bassford that I should have a piece of it. Everybody thought I was absolutely crazy! Lou Coit, who worked for Kipplinger, was a neighbor and friend, and he had advised me about some of my financial problems. He knew my "worth," as it were, and warned,

"Emily, you can't possibly afford it!"

All of my family thought I'd taken leave of my senses. After one visit to Maryland, my South Carolina family was aghast. They warned,

"You will never get that smell out of the house!"

Even John was very dubious about it, because he was not a bit well by that time. However, none of that stopped me, because I really thought I could do something with the place, if somehow I could just buy it!

When I spoke to Estep Gott about Obligation he said,

"I think you ought to buy Obligation and fix it up instead of trying to do anything with Old Place."

Estep was the only person who gave me any encouragement at all, and offered,

"I will lend you what you need to fix it up, and will buy back from you the 40 acres adjoining my place."

So we worked out a deal. Eas loaned me the money to buy a good part of the property, and I sold him enough land to get it paid off. That is the only way I could have held onto it, I guess. We made an offer of $20,000 to purchase the property which was eventually accepted.

We don't have all the information about Obligation that we might wish because so many of the records were lost. For some reason there were Stockett and other papers stored at Ivy Neck, Forbes Calhoun's lovely old house down on the Rhode River. Forbes had been persuaded, finally, to take the papers to the Hall of Records in Annapolis for safekeeping. Just a week before he was scheduled to do it, his house burned and the papers with it. Even so, there are still a good many references to Obligation in the Hall of Records, but nothing as complete as we would like. Thomas

Larkin, who lived across the road at Larkin's Hills, signed the original survey for the place. According to the record, the Legislature met at Larkin's Hills in 1665 or 1666. Larkin's Hills was a small gambrell-roofed house, and we think there was a similar house at Obligation. It appears that the house went through at least two transitions, and then sometime in the last century, probably about 1870, the roof was raised, and a third story added. Additionally, during this renovation the double chimneys on the ends of the structure were joined to exit the house as a single chimney on each end. The shape of the original structure can be seen in the different colors of the bricks on the exterior of the house walls.

One of the luckiest things that ever happened was when I met Miss Kathleen Cowgill. We had hired Archie Roger's firm as architects for Obligation. Archie had inherited a lovely old house north of Annapolis called Belvoir. His mother was quite a gardener, and her friend, Miss Cowgill, was really the smartest person I ever knew as far as landscape design is concerned. She lived on a farm near Easton where she had a small nursery, and we got her to come over to look at Obligation before we started doing anything. She was quite an unusual-looking character. She wore puttees and pants, and her hair was done up in a hairnet. She was very quiet and unassuming, and she would just stand and observe. Then she would announce a decision. It was Miss Cowgill who decided that we should change the entrance road, which originally came across the south yard, to approach the house from the north. She designed the driveway, the teardrop-shaped drive in front, and determined that we should change the three terraces into two.

She decided that we should push the lower terrace out to make the yard wider. We had a professional with a bulldozer do the work while she supervised. He pushed around a lot of dirt, and after he was finished, Miss Cowgill said,

"You need some flower beds out here."

But I decided that I had enough to do without caring for flower beds, and we wanted a nice green lawn. I didn't lay out the garden or buy boxwoods, because it seemed to be too much to take care of at the time.

Miss Cowgill and I got to be good friends. She would frequently spend the night with me, because she was also doing work in the neighborhood for some of my friends. About ten years after her original visit to Obligation, I asked,

"I want you to tell me what I should do with the front. I'm rather bored with it."

"I told you ten years ago. Why didn't you do it then?" she retorted.

"Better late than never," I decided, and we got some small box bushes and put them around in the square and started on the garden. Miss Cowgill brought over some of the shrubs from her nursery.

After we had rebuilt the entrance road so that it was suitable for automobiles, we got to work on the fields. We tried to clear one field each year. We still had a growth of scrub stuff between the highway and the entrance road. Of course, no one had put lime on the place in twenty years; broom sage was in the undergrowth, and there were no fences. The gullies were so deep you couldn't drive a tractor through a field. In the front, the field was particularly rugged with some high and steep hills. Instead of just cleaning out the field, we put screens around some of the larger tulip poplar trees. I was determined to keep some of them, along with the dogwoods, and I knew that without the fences, any tenants would just plow them up to put the land into tobacco. Any people that we approached to work the farm took one look at the fields and the cleaning out of the hedgerows expected of them, and declined the job.

The house we call the Red House was built in the 1920's, but it was nearly falling down. The former tenants had used some of the weatherboarding for kindling, and the roof was leaking. The man we hired to rebuild the house said that it was built like a barn with very heavy timbers, and the timbers were all that saved it. Inside and outside it was very ugly, but we needed to repair the house for the tenant to live in. So at the same time we were trying to get the fields cleared, we were making repairs on the Red House, and Obligation still stood empty.

Finally, we were successful at finding a tenant for the property. The first tenant was financed through the farm financing program, and I signed a note guaranteeing him so much money a month until the tobacco crop was sold. We planted only a small crop of tobacco, but when we harvested, our barn was filled. We didn't have any tractor then, and we had trouble satisfying this tenant with the horses we bought. Each time we bought a horse, the tenant would decide it wasn't the right kind, and he'd return it. We finally figured out that he had an arrangement with the stable owner, so that each time one horse was returned and another sold, the tenant received a commission.

On the first of January, the tenant came to me and said, "I'm sorry, but I have to leave."

Here I was with a barn full of tobacco needing to be stripped, and all the money I'd borrowed to back him with was gone! I tried to sell the crop to one of the tobacco sales companies, but they didn't offer enough to take care of the debt. Finally I was able to get some of my patients to come and strip out the tobacco, then took it to the market myself with a Jeep and a trailer. When I reached the tobacco barn, I needed to ask for help to back up the trailer so it could be unloaded.

The biggest problem was always the tenants ... finding good ones and keeping them. The landowner furnished the tenant a house and the land and some of the equipment, although many of the better tenants had their own tools. A financial deal with the tenant was fixed by the first of December each year. The landowner and tenant agreed upon an amount of money which would be advanced the tenant monthly. Some tenants had jobs on the side and didn't need as much of a draw, but very few tenants were able to save enough capital to carry themselves through the year until the tobacco crop was sold. Tobacco was almost the only crop that either of us got any money from, and it was sold only once a year. There was a bill of sale on the crop from the time it was planted, and this amount was deducted from the amount owed the tenant from the eventual sale price of the crop.

In the winter, the main activity was to strip the tobacco hanging in the barn. The tobacco was taken from the barn and put in the stripping room when the weather was propitious; that is, it had to be damp so that the tobacco didn't crumble. The stripping room in the new barn was very nice and cozy because there was a wood stove and chimney, so stripping the tobacco became a social activity. The tenant family sat around the stove and passed a stalk of tobacco from one person to the next. One person would strip off the bottom leaves, and the next would strip off the top leaves. Often each person would have a different color of tobacco to strip.

In the early days, the tobacco was put into "hogsheads," which were big barrels made on the farms. It was shipped to Baltimore to the market, which was the only market around for a long time. About the time we moved from Old Place, they opened the "loose-leaf market" in Upper Marlboro, and shortly afterward they began to hold markets in various locations in southern Maryland. This made the selling season last nearly all summer, and the buyers would go on a circuit from South Carolina to North Carolina to Virginia, where at each place they bought a different kind of tobacco. In southern Maryland, we had a very special kind of tobacco that was said to have higher burning power for cigarettes. The best tobacco was frequently exported to Europe, but it was a very uncertain market, and farmers thought the buyers got together the night before the market opened to agree on a price.

Farming problems were an irritant to me. I could become very impatient about a problem at the office, or be upset about a patient being very ill, and then come home to find the tractor broken down or the tenant gone on a binge. Willie, the best tenant I ever had, was a very good worker. Every month he took his monthly check, cashed it at the liquor store, and then he would not only drink a little, but he would proceed to get absolutely plastered!

Willie lived with another couple who had quite a number of children. They all seemed to get along until he gave in to this periodic weakness. The family members were afraid of him when he started to drink because he was ready to destroy everything and everybody, but Willie never once came anywhere near me when he was drunk.

The police knew Willie quite well, and I finally made a deal with the police Captain. I suggested, "Now, when you see Willie drunk on the side of the road, just pick him up, take him down to the jail and keep him overnight. In the morning, after he sobers up, I'll come and get him out, and we'll start over." That went on for four or five years until Willie went on one binge too many. One night at Woodland Beach, he climbed into an abandoned car in the parking lot, and fell asleep with a lighted cigarette in his mouth. Eventually both Willie and the inside of the car caught on fire. When the police called me, I said, "I'll be down to get him in a little while."

"No hurry, doctor. We just want you to identify him," they answered, "because he's dead."

John began to realize that we were going to have to come to some decision about Old Place. I've always regretted allowing him to do it. There were two halves to the property, an Upper Farm and a Lower Farm. Ike Shepherd was pressing him to buy part of the farm, so John decided to sell him half of the Lower Farm. We had built a new barn, a new tenant house, and had fixed up another house on those 600 acres. John sat down and figured out some costs, but I never knew where he got his figures. Unfortunately, John completely underestimated what he should get for it, and he sold nearly 300 acres for just over $10,000! With this money we paid off the remaining debt to the Wilson heirs.

John's health and the absence of decent tenants caused the sale of the remainder of the farm. We had tried working it for several years, but it became hopeless. I talked to Eas about it, and he agreed that we should sell it. It nearly broke my heart because it had been in John's family for all those years. We got $38,000 for it, which was nothing. That same half of the farm has been on the market for as much as $1.5 million.

# THIRTY-ONE

*I've heard that it was through Dr. Wilson that Dr. Aris Allen
got on the hospital Staff. I know both of her sons very well, and
I remember Mr. John Wilson. He was a wonderful man.*

Sam Pratt

I had been on the Staff of the hospital for 22 years - ever since I
forced the issue after arriving in Anne Arundel County. To my
great surprise, I was elected Chief of Staff in 1951. I certainly did-
n't campaign for the job, but I think they elected me because of the
contention on the Staff. I was the only person all of them spoke to.
The Staff was preparing to write new bylaws at that time, and
there were verbal floor fights at nearly every meeting! The reason
for such rancor was that the hospital Staff was about to divide into
medical specialist services. Although there were doctors who were
considered medical specialists when I was in medical school, they
were rare.

There came a time at the hospital in Annapolis when over-
crowded conditions made expansion necessary. John Rich, the
nephew of Mr. Summerfield Baldwin and the manager of Mr.
Baldwin's finances, offered an endowment of $2 million to the hos-
pital if we could raise matching funds to build a new hospital
wing. There was a contingency to his generosity: Mr. Baldwin
insisted the doctors of the hospital Staff be divided into medical
services. John Rich came to the Staff meetings to lay down the law:

"Now, you all understand that Mr. Baldwin insists that we find
a prominent surgeon to come down to run this Surgery; and that
we get an outstanding man as Chief of Medicine; and that we hire
a Somebody as Chief of Pediatrics!" he thundered, thumping on
the table.

This caused a tremendous amount of friction because many doctors were accustomed to doing their own surgery and felt they
were being insulted or that their livelihood was being taken away.
The doctors felt it was an intrusion for a lay person to tell them
what they could or could not do, and that stirred up the ire among
the Staff. However, mindful of the need for a larger hospital, the
hospital board brought specialists from Johns Hopkins to head the
various departments of the hospital, including Surgery.

During the fracas with the hospital staff, I encountered John
Rich at a cocktail party at Tulip Hill. He was by that time the head
of the hospital board. I'd had a drink and was feeling very brave.

"You know," I declared, "I want to tell you that I think you are

101

the greatest son of a bitch I have ever known in my life!"

He looked at me and said, "Emily, I have been waiting for somebody to tell me that for at least a year! Let's go back to your house and talk about it."

So we returned to Obligation and sat down and talked the rest of the evening about what was going on at the hospital, and we were able to reach an understanding.

When we held the groundbreaking ceremony for the new wing, Mr. Summerfield Baldwin removed the first shovel-full of dirt with a bulldozer. Governor McKeldin attended, and in my capacity as Chief of Staff, I was scheduled to make a speech. The Hon. William McWilliams, a judge on the Court of Appeals, later joked that he had put my speech into English for me. However, even as we broke ground for the new wing, we realized that it would be outgrown by the time it was completed, and it was.

At about the same time as the reorganization of the hospital, the American Medical Association decided that general practitioners should organize themselves in order to gain more status or prestige. This was undoubtedly a result of the movement into fields of specialization by most of the medical commmunity. Groups of general practitioners were forming throughout the country. Dr. Guyther, who practiced all his life in St. Mary's County, started the organization in St. Mary's, but I was the one who began it in this area. Several of us general practitioners got together and formed the Academy of General Practice in Southern Maryland. One thing we accomplished was to help build the hospital in LaPlata. I had met Mrs. Julia Wills when I was dealing with hospital politics and just as we expanded into the Baldwin Wing. She and her husband, James, wanted to build a hospital in LaPlata. I invited the Wills' and the doctors from LaPlata to meet at Obligation with our hospital administrator and staff. We helped them get organized, and they did build a very nice hospital in LaPlata. Fortunately, Mrs. Wills was able to do it when she did, because not long afterward she developed cancer.

The hospital Staff had almost finished rewriting the bylaws when I was reelected to another term as Chief of Staff. Unfortunately, the violent verbal arguments became too big a nuisance, added to worrying about John's health, my practice, and the farms. In the middle of my second term, I asked Dr. Robert Welch, Sr., to complete my term of office. Dr. Welch came from a family of doctors and everybody on the staff liked him. He also had great presence and was a fine looking man. To my great relief, he agreed to complete my second term.

After leaving as Chief of Staff of the hospital, I was elected President of the County Medical Society and served in that position for two years. The business of the County Medical Society is to promulgate rules for the practice of medicine in the county and to vote on doctors applying for membership. You get more literature from the state medical and chirurgical faculties than you can put in a trash basket!

When I first came to the county, the County Medical Society had only 17 members, and more than half of those were either at Crownsville or the Naval Academy. There were very few in private practice. By the late 1940's when they reorganized the hospital Staff, there were about 45 doctors; and, although segregation remained well into the 1960's, several black doctors were already on the hospital Staff. Dr. Johnson had his own clinic with a large practice. I treated his wife when she attempted suicide. Dr. Richardson was a very nice old doctor who was very good about taking care of my home deliveries if any happened to be due while I was away. I also worked with a Dr. Cook at times.

Dr. Aris Allen and Mrs. Allen, a physician in her own right, were a wonderful pair of very intelligent people. They had joint offices, and Aris Allen really eased some of the problems we'd had with a few black doctors. Dr. Allen was an outstanding example to his people and to the whole community. He was so well thought of that he became the Chief of Staff of the hospital. He saw both black and white patients, and he vaccinated me once when I had allowed my passport to expire. I was on my way to Europe, and Virginia Meredith, who was secretary to Dr. Beard, the County Health Officer, had said she would stamp the passport for me if I could get someone to vaccinate me. Dr. Allen happened to be in his office that day, and he vaccinated me on the spot. We were great friends, and he attended several parties at my home. He served as Master of Ceremonies at the party given for me when I had completed 50 years of practice, and I attended the memorial service for Dr. Allen when a statue was erected in his honor.

There was almost more Jim Crow in Maryland than there was in the South. The quarterly meetings of the County Medical Society were evening dinner meetings. It was very hard to find a place where our black doctors were accepted. We were a comparatively small group, because half the doctors never attended meetings, anyway. Carvel Hall was just about the only place that would permit us to include black people, so we held most of our dinners there. Education and the Civil Rights Movement has changed much of that nonsense for the better.

# THIRTY-TWO

*God knows, the house and farm are monuments to her energy.*
*It was barely four walls and a roof.*

Christopher H. Wilson

Finally, Eas Gott announced that we would have to get Obligation ready for occupancy because he was ready to retire and move down to Etowah. Archie Rogers' partner in charge of our project was Frank Taliaferro; and although he went on to become quite famous with offices in New Zealand and Texas, for instance, it was his first job. He didn't seem to know any more about what he was doing than I did.

Even after we'd shoveled out the rubble left by the squatters, the house still reeked. We took the house completely apart down to the bricks. There were one or two places where we were able to leave some of the plaster, but that turned out to be a mistake. The original plaster had been put directly on the bricks, and the moisture seeped through, causing the plaster and paint eventually to peel and disintegrate. It has caused a problem over the years.

Since Obligation's interior walls are solid brick, in order to install the electricity and plumbing upstairs, we had to take out the chimney cupboards in the living room and run the pipes and electric lines up the walls and then replace the chimney cupboards. The electric lines had to be channeled into the bricks throughout the house. Later on, they installed the air conditioning the same way, and later still when our thermostat failed, it was necessary to do an entirely new job because it's impossible to pull the wires out to replace them. I've learned a whole lot about old houses!

Eas Gott undertook to supervise most of the work on the house. We would never have finished it without him, and he saved us from a lot of mistakes. As it turned out, we needed to make very few structural changes. The roof was only about ten years old, and the floors were original. Fortunately, no one had undertaken any previous restoration ... sometimes old houses are ruined by doing too much. We cut a door from the parlor to the den to open up the lower floor. It was Eas' idea that we make two bathrooms by dividing the only upstairs room without a fireplace. He also suggested that we use a strip of a wall to build two walk-in closets because there were no closets anywhere in the house. One closet opens into the master bedroom and one into the guest bedroom. Aside from that, we didn't make any changes. We didn't do anything with the third floor for about ten years when we made the one large room into two bedrooms and a bath.

We had a little difficulty deciding on which of the downstairs rooms to use for the kitchen. At first, we thought to make the den into the kitchen, closing up the fireplace in the process. The workmen had already completed the channels for the electric lines when Eas determined that the corner fireplace in the den is a unique feature of the house. I decided that we shouldn't destroy this very early fireplace, and we installed the kitchen in a room across the hall from the den, but the electrical outlets in the den remain at counter height to this day. Some of the chair railing we removed from the kitchen was usable, so it was hung in the dining room; and Dick Hartge then made new moldings for the living room and the cornices for the windows. Although most of the woodwork in the house is original, he reconstructed the battered woodwork throughout the house. The canopy over the South entrance was also designed and built by Dick Hartge. It is a copy of the one at Tulip Hill, except that we asked Dick to carve a maple leaf rather than a tulip poplar bud as the trim.

For $50 we bought a derelict house to obtain some floor boards, old bricks and a few oak sills to use at Obligation. We bought some locks for the doors from a black family living in an old house in Owensville. The locks were all in pieces, but I found a place in Baltimore that would repair them. Although the locks weren't nearly as old as the house, they date to 1840 or 1850. They carry the manufacturer's name "Carpenter," and we think they were made in England.

Porches had been built on each side of the house in the 1920's, making the interior of the house very dark. The former owners had whitewashed the bricks under the porches. After we had removed the porches, we had the most awful mess trying to get the paint off the brick. We tried fuming nitric acid, but we finally had to scrape it off by hand. One of my friends came by after we got things pretty straight, and asked,

"Why did you put in all of those new bricks?"

Of course, there wasn't a new brick in the place. I recently read that Ross Perot had a similar problem and solved it by having each brick reversed to hide the painted side. I didn't have money enough to do that even if we'd thought of it.

At the North entrance only a small wooden step served as an entry, and the basement entrance door was very low. This made the house appear to be sitting under a hill. We dug out that north basement room, and, because the floors in the basement were all dirt, we then poured cement floors throughout. We were able to get some large handmade bricks from St. James Church ... leftovers from the wall Mr. Chewning was building around the churchyard. With these bricks, we constructed the entrance steps and the small porch over the basement entrance. Then Edwin H. Gott, Eas' nephew, designed and built the decorative iron gates for the basement door. (He later became Chairman of the Board of U.S. Steel.)

It seemed to take forever for the contractors to get finished with the house. When they began the project, they had informed us that it would take only about six weeks to finish the job. As time went on, they'd work for a while, and then the electrician or plumber wouldn't show up and no work would be done for a week or more. In March 1951, I finally had to tell the contractors to finish up because we were going to occupy the house in exactly one month whether they were finished or not. I think I stirred them up because they finished everything except for sanding the floors. They might still be working on the house if I hadn't put my foot down.

On April 1, 1951, John went to work as usual. It was near the end of his working life, and he was not at all well. He had been dreading for weeks the process of moving and exactly how it was going to be accomplished. I didn't say anything to him, but I had alerted all the help from Etowah and Obligation; and, after John left the house, they hitched the horses and the tractor to the wagons. When they arrived at Etowah, we packed up all the china and glass, loaded everything on the wagons, and then drove the whole caravan across the fields to Obligation! By the time John returned in the evening, we had the furniture in place, all the beds made, and dinner ready.

I had bought a great big steak in celebration of getting into our house. In those days, steak was still pretty rare. Gladys Reed, our wonderful cook, was down on all fours fixing the rug in the dining room. When our big boxer dog asked to be let out, she reached up and opened the door for him. Instantly she glimpsed out of the corner of her eye that the dog had taken our steak from the counter and had it firmly clamped in his jaws. Gladys chased him into the yard, wrestled the steak away from him, brought it back into the house, washed it off, and we ate it for dinner!

# THIRTY-THREE

After his heart attack in Maine in 1946, John continued to work at the Comptroller's Office in Annapolis every day. Tilden Atwell, who was also in that office, remembers that John had a very heavy cough, and would, nevertheless, roll his own cigarettes at his desk, coughing all the while and dropping tobacco all over his clothes.

John succeeded in working for perhaps another six months after we moved into Obligation. Finally, he had to be brought home from his office because he had become very breathless and there had been some heart failure. He never went back to work.

He was bedridden here at the house for nearly a year before he died. We put a bed in the den for him, and I had nurses around the clock. Many times I never knew when I went out on call whether John would be here when I got home. It was very difficult to see him waste away to nothing. One June day in 1951, we stayed by his bedside, thinking that day would be his last. It turned out that he had developed pneumonia, and if we hadn't had penicillen, he'd surely have gone then.

He rallied for a time, but one morning in January 1952, when the nurse went to his room to give him his breakfast, he was gone. He was 67 years old, and we'd had nearly 20 years together.

John and Chris had realized that their father's health was precarious, but Chris at 16 years of age took John's death particularly hard. He had always been extremely close to his father, and John's death traumatized him for quite a while.

John's funeral and burial were at St. James Church. It was a big funeral. The Gotts came down from Pittsburgh, and John's mother, his sisters and a brother-in-law were there. John's mother eventually outlived all of her children.

I was grateful that I had my practice to occupy my days, and I needed to work because we didn't have any money. Although John had worked 30 years for the State of Maryland, the only compensation he received was $900 in severance pay for vacations he hadn't taken. There was no pension system in those days. There were some strenuous times finding the money to pay for John in his second year at Princeton and for Chris at Friend's School in Baltimore. The boys would come home off and on during their breaks from classes, and that helped make my life less lonely.

It was determined that Chris needed some professional help, and after much trial and error, we found a remarkable young man who recommended a school in Pleasantville, New Jersey. This school promised individual instruction to each child, but it was horrendously expensive! It cost $1,000 a month, plus all the extras. My patient and friend, Howard Atterbury, who had been so instrumental in obtaining John's scholarship to Hill, had left me a few bonds. "So," I determined, "if that will do it, we'll use them." Chris hated the school, of course. Every time I took him back to New Jersey, I nearly had to put a rope around his neck and drag him there; but it did the job, thank God, and they got him to pass.

Later, to my great surprise and pleasure, Chris came to me and asked, "If I can get into the University of Virginia, will you pay my tuition?" Chris passed the entrance exams and loved it from the day he entered. I think he would be there still if I hadn't stopped paying his tuition. He was elected to the best fraternity on campus and spent a lot of time running it ... actually, a little too much time...but he made some wonderful and lasting friendships.

John had thought he would like to study medicine, but organic chemistry defeated him, and he flunked it twice. After he finished at Princeton in 1954, he joined the Air Force and served three years. When he came home, he got a job in the trust department at the Riggs Bank. Most of the people in that department had law degrees, and the bank sent John to law school at night. After two years, he quit his job and went to law school full time at the University of Maryland in Baltimore. There he met Jon Frisby, who was a teacher and counselor, and they shared an apartment on Charles Street while he was going to school. During the summers, John clerked for Mr. William Kelly's law firm, and after he passed the bar, he got a job in the firm through Mr. Kelly who lives at Sudley. He commuted from Obligation to Washington for 25 years.

My practice at the Tea House continued to increase. We saw many Medicare patients and as many black people as white people. We didn't turn anyone away, and we tried to find financial assistance for those who had no means to pay for services. I became irritated when I knew a patient had the means to pay bills but didn't. The staff reported that thousands and thousands of dollars owed me were never collected. The nurses kindly said that I was not difficult to work for, but they complained that I habitually confused the files and in my haste called patients out of proper sequence. The Tea House yard was full of parked cars and the overflow was parked down along the edge of Rt. 2. The telephone rang continually, and it was a hectic four-hour clip for us twice a day while we churned through appointments and emergencies. The lab space was tiny, and the examining room was small with only a curtain for privacy. The nurses were a great help to me because in addition to their professional expertise, they were personally acquainted with nearly every patient we saw, and their knowledge of family connections sometimes helped me with diagnoses. On the other hand, because of their personal friendship with the patients and knowledge of their illnesses, the nurses often paid an emotional price.

In addition to office hours, I continued to visit patients in their homes, especially elderly patients, and went to the hospital each day in the afternoon to check on others. On Tuesdays I attended the childrens' clinics in Davidsonville and Churchton, and the nurses had a job getting me to leave the office on time. Saturdays were especially difficult for me, when I had personal errands and farm problems to attend to and when I checked on hospital patients. We tried to find some doctors who would agree to fill in part time so that I could get away from the practice. They would come for one day at a time, and it seemed they were always late. In fact, Margie Moreland was in the habit of telephoning any doctor who hadn't arrived at the office, sometimes getting him out of bed! Dr. Wilkins came from Annapolis for some evening office hours, and Dr. Church and Dr. Linhardt, the County Medical Examiner, both helped us out. On days when he was late, Dr. Church would fling open the Tea House door and exclaim,

"I'm racing the rats this morning!"

While they were senior medical students, John Seible and William Hall, Jr., gave me relief while they got experience. Doctors saw things in country practice that they would never see in Annapolis!

For a while I dated Ed Rich, the younger brother of John Rich. Ed had a very different personality from his brother. He was a quiet and private person and very relaxed. Ed's wife had walked off leaving him with two little children to raise. Although I never knew her, I knew that she had treated him very badly. By the time I knew Ed, she had died and their children were grown and married. Ed drove a dilapidated Buick, although he could have afforded anything. He drove that car very slowly ... so slowly, in fact, that once on his way down to see me, he was stopped by a policeman on the South River Bridge for being a traffic hazard. Although I liked Ed very much, we eventually decided that a marriage between us was not in the cards.

The 1950's and 1960's were very dynamic years in this neighborhood. Obligation has always embraced any family member who, for some reason, might run onto hard times. From time to time, people needing "time out" arrived for extended visits. Of course, there was so much work to do on the place that they were expected to pitch in. As busy as I was, I enjoyed a goodly amount of visiting back and forth and cocktail parties and other social events. Eas and Fran Gott had come to live at Etowah, and the Clagetts were living at Larkin's Hills. The Gotts held an open house in the summertime for family members from all over the country. Nearly everyone would visit at one time or another, and there seemed always to be something going on. Eas thought there was nothing better than opening Etowah to all the family, and Fran was a marvelous hostess who served wonderful meals. Eas redesigned and repaired a small cottage which we rented from Kirkpatrick Howat. It was down on the Rhode River ... just a simple little building where people could change clothes before swimming. There was a dock and a swimming area netted against sea nettles, and it was a popular place for the young people.

One year, all the Gotts came down, along with Eas' niece, Betty Templeton and her children from Chicago. We must have had twenty or thirty people here. We dug a pit out in the yard and roasted a whole lamb. Young John got up at 5:00 o'clock in the morning to start the coals. We rented tables and set them up on the lawn. It was beautiful weather, and we had quite a party. The only problem arose just before the lamb was ready, when John realized that he didn't know how to carve a whole lamb. He called Rookie's Market in Annapolis, and they sent out an apprentice butcher who carved the meat for us.

As Deputy Comptroller, John had worked under Mr. Tawes, who was elected Governor in 1958. After his election, Governor and Mrs. Tawes asked me to call on them at the Governor's Mansion, and I was asked to be Mrs. Tawes' doctor. She wasn't a sick person, fortunately, but she did have a little high blood pressure, so every month or so I took her blood pressure. I was invited to some of the state dinner parties from time to time. It was very complimentary.

# THIRTY-FOUR

*You know, every time you went to a party, you'd see this little*
*knot of men, and you could just be sure that Emily was right*
*in the middle of it.*

Sally Whall

In November 1956, I went to Europe on a medical studies trip sponsored by Duke University. It was my first trip to Europe, and my sister, Louise went with me. From a professional point of view, it was quite interesting because the Dean of the Medical School and a good many of the faculty were along. Each day a faculty member gave seminars on medical issues for which we received academic credits. We traveled on an Italian ship, and the food was absolutely fabulous! The ship made several stops in the Mediterranean, including Barcelona. From Barcelona we took a bus to visit the Shrine of the Black Virgin and bought some of the specialty liquor produced there by the monks. On the day we arrived in Venice, the city was in the middle of a sleet storm. I had always thought of Venice as having a semitropical climate, but certainly not that day!

We had only a 24-hour stay in Venice, then boarded the night train to Rome, and it was still cold. The two men who were in charge of our tour found a compartment and invited Louise and me to share it with them. We piled our coats on the end of the seats to discourage others from entering our compartment, and, in an attempt to keep warm during the long night ride, we drank the bottle of liquor we'd purchased near Barcelona.

We stayed a week in Rome at the Excelsior Hotel. We went to dinner at Alfredo's Restaurant, where Alfredo himself tossed our fettucini, and I was invited to use the gold knife and fork given the restaurant by Mary Pickford and Douglas Fairbanks.

When we arrived at the train station in Milan, we found a taxi and asked to be driven to the Covallo Hotel. The taxidriver didn't recognize that name. A representative of Louise's company in Milan didn't recognize it either, but suggested the Palace Hotel. We asked the desk clerk at the Palace to find out if we had any mail at the Covallo. He looked perfectly blank, and finally said, "That hotel was bombed out during the war and never rebuilt."

Our intention had been to spend the day in Milan because we especially wanted to see the fresco of the Last Supper in the monastery. However, another mix-up in our travel plans forced us to leave Milan at 10:00 the next morning. Just before train time, we hired a cab and rode around to look at the Cathedral and the

Opera House, then rushed to the monastery, begging at the door to be let in to glimpse the fresco. Unhappily, we were told we were too early and wouldn't be admitted. In a way, I was glad that we took the morning train because it went through the Alps, and the scenery was beautiful.

Louise and I ended our trip in Paris. Again, representatives of Louise's company met us at the train, taking us out to lunch at a restaurant on the Seine and acting as our private tour guides around the town. They had made reservations for dinner and the floor show at the Lido, and we were to be escorted by the manager of the office and two or three others.

In the meantime, I had to buy a dress to wear. (Louise said I never had the right clothes.) We went to a little shop where I found a very plain black dress formal enough to wear out to dinner. The dress needed some alteration, but when the salesgirl promised to have the dress at the hotel by 5:00 p.m, Louise and I returned to the hotel to rest before dinner. Five o'clock came and went, and the dress hadn't arrived. It got later and later, and our escorts were coming for us at 6:30. At the last possible moment the dress was delivered, the gentlemen arrived, and we went off to the Lido. We had a ringside table, right on the walkway, and ate our dinner watching the floor show. There we were ... close enough to touch all those gals who were wearing nothing from the waist up ... and not too much from the waist down, either. I was a little concerned about Louise, because she had never married and had lived a rather sheltered life, and our escorts made jokes about "fried eggs." But we were drinking champagne, and it seemed to loosen Louise up a whole lot!

After the floor show we danced and were having such a good time that we decided to stay for the late show. Afterward, although we were becoming a bit tired, our hosts announced, "Now, we're going to go out for breakfast." We went to the cellar at the George V, where we listened to Spanish music. I had French onion soup for breakfast, but Louise settled for scrambled eggs.

Since our travels occurred during the Suez crisis, taxis in Paris were pretty hard to come by. The office manager and his friends lived out in the suburbs of Paris; so Louise and I offered, bigheartedly, to walk back to our hotel so that our escorts could take the taxi. We walked back from the George V at 5:00 in the morning and noticed that it had snowed a little bit while we were partying ... just enough to look pretty. When we found ourselves walking by the Church of the Madeleine, we decided we'd go to early Mass before we went to bed. However, the church doors were locked, so we just sat on the steps and waited until they opened at 6:00 a.m.

Our plan for the day was to go to the matinee at the Opera, and

Louise began agitating about 11:00 in the morning, urging me to get up.

"Come on, now, we've got to get dressed."

I groaned, "I don't think I can make it."

But Louise said, "We aren't going to be in Paris again, so get up and let's go!"

We saw a remarkable and wonderful production of Faust. The actors dancing in Hell on stage seemed quite apropos in light of the evening we had spent at the Lido.

We were away about three weeks, and if we had known enough, and if we'd had the option, we might have taken the plane to Europe returning by ship, instead of the other way 'round. We'd taken a lot of clothing, because it was necessary to dress for dinner on the ship, and we'd made some substantial purchases. In those days, there were no jet airplanes, and it was necessary to weigh all airplane baggage carefully. When we took our suitcases to be weighed, we found it would cost $50 extra to take them on our plane, so we packed them firmly and sent them home by ship.

# THIRTY-FIVE

When I first arrived in southern Maryland, the only Catholic Church anywhere around was a tiny wooden chapel, Our Lady of Sorrows, in Owensville. It was a mission from St. Mary's in Annapolis, and the Redemptorist Priests came on Sundays and Saints' Days to say Mass, but we had no resident priest. The congregation consisted of perhaps ten families altogether. We remained a very small group until people from Washington realized they could commute to work and began to winterize the cottages built on the beaches. Shady Side and all of the other little communities started to grow.

Mrs. Flather, who owned Tulip Hill, was a Catholic. She was a very wealthy woman, and she had fixed up the old church a little by enlarging the original building and by adding stained glass windows. However, the congregation, which also included the Davidsonville area, was growing very rapidly.

Just about the time the size of the old church had reached crisis proportions, Bennett Darnall's father died leaving Bennett all his money. He also left a fund which was dedicated to help finance the construction of a new church. Bennett announced he would give the new church in memory of his mother and father, but only on the condition that the Bishop would send a resident priest to Owensville. The Darnalls wanted a suitable Pastor who would make a good impression on the neighborhood. The Redemptorists, in the first place, were a little reluctant to give up their interest in the church, but when they finally agreed, Bennett and his wife, Anne, assumed control of the construction. It became Bennett's retirement project, and I'm sure he added money to the amount Mr. Darnall had left. Since I was a close friend of the Darnall's, I became very familiar with all of the problems they encountered.

They put a great deal of love and care into building the church, hiring Robbie Robbins, a famous New York architect. All three went to Williamsburg and were inspired by one of the renovated churches there. Robbie drew the plan for the new Our Lady of Sorrows using the Williamsburg church as a guide. He traveled to Owensville from New York several times to supervise the construction of the building. The influence of Williamsburg is evident in the handmade bricks and blown glass window panes. The figure of the Madonna above the altar represents Our Lady of Walsingham, a replica of an old English shrine where women desiring to have children went to pray.

The congregation was very proud of their new church. The

pews were beautiful and the center aisle was wide. The old church had only a center aisle, but the new one had room for side aisles, and they have been a lifesaver. Bennett decided that he and Anne would claim the two front seats on the left side of the center aisle, and I was assigned the front seat on the right side, but this arrangement didn't last too long. That's fine with me, because I would much rather sit toward the back.

The congregation was very fortunate because Bennett gave the entire building, and then he gave the Rectory. The congregation finally built the Hall, but we were lucky because that was a comparatively small contribution. Our Parish must consist of 800 families now. We have four Masses every Sunday, and they are all crowded, and we've really outgrown the church again. A few years ago there was some discussion about enlarging the church by adding space on the back. The older crowd, of which I am one, protested, arguing that it shouldn't be spoiled.

Bennett Darnall lived at Portland Manor. Originally named Allendale, the property was one of the grants of ten thousand-acre manors granted by the Lord Proprietors. The original grant was to the Gott family, and tradition says that one of the Gotts lost Allendale to a Darnall in a card game. Since the Darnall's holdings were named Portland Manor, Allendale assumed that name. (Now owned by Harry and Betty Ford, the house has been restored, and the yard contains beautiful box gardens and very old trees.)

Bennett's first wife died of cancer before I came down to the country, and they'd had no children. He was a well-to-do lawyer from Baltimore who, before his retirement, commuted to Portland Manor on weekends. They entertained very lavishly. He furnished shotgun shells to his tenants who then hunted the quail to be served at their elegant dinners. The quail was frequently preceded by diamond-back terrapin soup. His second wife was his secretary, Anne Eugenia Brown. Although they had been very anxious for a child, they also were unable to have children. She took charge of the altar linens for the church and saw that the brasses were polished. Anne was a perfectionist. She didn't want anybody to change anything she had done, and she especially didn't like it when a newcomer was seated on the front pew of the church. To her mind it was a social faux pas and simply "not done."

Both Bennett and Anne were my patients. When Bennett was in his early 70's, his health began to fail. His heart was a problem and he had terrific anemia, the cause of which eluded us. I had consulted Dr. Ben Rutledge of Hopkins who came down occasionally to see Bennett, and we finally had to put Bennett in an oxygen tent. One day, after I had driven Chris to school, Bennett asked his nurse to call me because Anne was out of the house. Bennett was conscious enough to know he needed us, and as soon as Ben Rutledge looked at him, Ben ordered him into the hospital. We called an ambulance, and about the time it arrived, Anne drove up. She convinced herself that we had snatched Bennett out from under her control and flew into a fury, declaring, "If you take him out of that door, I will not pay any of your bills!" Anne had assumed financial control because of Bennett's illness.

"Well, I don't give a damn!" Ben Rutledge stormed, "He's got to go."

At the hospital they found Bennett had an ulcer, among other things. I don't know why they couldn't have given him enough blood, but they couldn't, and he died two days later.

Anne had become a manic depressive, and also had begun to drink more than she should. Her lawyer at the time was James Morton. She called Morton and asked him to call Hampton MacGruder and me and order us not to come to the funeral. I'd never before been uninvited to a funeral! I didn't attend, thinking I might be removed by the police, but Hampton was one of Bennett's boyhood friends, and they had attended Georgetown University together.

"Hell!" Hamp thought. "I've known Bennett longer than she has." He went to the funeral, and as she was leaving the church, Anne stopped, shook hands with Hamp, and thanked him for coming!

Bennett was buried in the churchyard. Because the Darnalls had been so instrumental in establishing the independent parish and separating from St. Mary's, Anne thought the priest was there to do her bidding. After an argument over some minor thing with the new young priest who had moved into the Rectory, Anne went to the Archbishop and demanded that the priest be removed. When her request was denied, she announced,

"Well, if you are not going to do what I ask, I am going to move Bennett to Baltimore." She bought a lot in a new cemetery in Baltimore, hired a truck, exhumed Bennett, and took him up to Baltimore where he was reburied. But I know that Bennett would have wanted to stay at Our Lady of Sorrows.

For obvious reasons, I was unable to participate in any of the women's groups of the times, but one very hot summer I did invite the church women to hold their meeting at Obligation. John and Chris, as they described it to me later, were outside playing badminton one afternoon, when all of a sudden several cars began arriving. A group of ladies got out of the cars, and seeing the boys, one asked,

"Is your mother here?"

"No," John answered, "she is probably still at the office."

"Oh, we were supposed to have our meeting here today."

"Fine. That's OK, come on in," the boys invited.

John and Chris hurried down to the freezer in the basement and found some pound cake and some of their Aunt Katharine's fruitcake. They cut the pound cake slices into quarters to make it appear plentiful and also fixed some soft drinks. They passed everything around and, making sure their guests were taken care of, they went back to their game. After a while, imagining that I had been held up by some medical emergency, the women decided to begin their meeting without me. They were about halfway through it, when I drove up.

"What's going on?" I asked. I had forgotten all about the meeting, and after my office hours I'd gone to The Lord's Bounty to swim in the Coit's pool!

# THIRTY-SIX

*Everybody was her patient. I know of only a few people who weren't.*

*Sally Whall*

By the 1960's, I had been practicing in the county for 30 years. I had a great number of patients and was very busy at the hospital and with the farm, and somewhere along the line I had become the Assistant County Medical Examiner. My sons were educated and living their own lives. After law school, John lived here in the house for about a year while we fixed up the Red House for him and Jon Frisby. Chris, after one early annulled marriage, married his childhood sweetheart, and bought a "fixer-upper" house in Howard County. They finished it just before their son, John, was born. Bettie and Chris lived in Howard County for about five years, and then decided that they, too, wanted to come back to Obligation to live; so I gave them five acres of land on which they built their house.

My normal day during this period was to get up early, have breakfast, and then try to get something done in the garden before going to work. I liked to get to the Tea House a little ahead of the staff, but they, in turn, wanted to arrive before I did. They said they had to work to stay one step ahead of me because I was never late. The office staff became a very close-knit group and did their best to protect me because they saw that I was so busy. Although I continued to see pre-natal cases, I had to stop home deliveries in the 1960's because they had begun to interfere with the regular patient case load.

I had trained the staff that it was better to be safe than sorry, and let them know that 80% of heart patients might live if they got to the hospital within a half hour of the first symptoms. Early one Saturday before Dr. Linhardt arrived to take office hours, Margie Moreland was alone in the office when a man in obvious distress arrived to see the doctor. Although she was not a nurse, Margie called the ambulance immediately without waiting for a doctor's approval. It was a good thing she did!

After office hours and hospital rounds, I might be lucky enough to get home in time to see what was going on at the farm before my dinner. A good part of the time, I didn't have any satisfactory help on the farm or anyone to fix meals. Three nights a week, I had office hours from about 6:30 "til finished," which was usually about 9:00 p.m.

Cory Cramer, a recent widower originally from Chicago, was living and working as a yacht broker in Annapolis. His wife had been his lifeline, and I think he missed her very much. He became very attentive to me. He gave me a flower every day for at least a year and insisted on taking me out to dinner every night. I would get home after nine o'clock, so tired I wanted only to go to bed, but Cory would say,

"Now, tonight we are going up to Busch's Restaurant (or somewhere else) for dinner."

He wanted to be here every night, and most of the time he'd say he wanted dinner, and most of the time I didn't have any cook, so most of the time we did go out. There was no getting away from it, which was one of the problems. Cory had a very nice house on Crab Creek, just beyond Maryland Road and up a little hill overlooking the water, where he kept a sailboat. Frequently, we had supper at his house with some of his friends, served by the good maid who had been with his wife when she was alive. He would have married me at any time, but I was somewhat involved in a triangle, and I couldn't seem to make a decision. Although we were very friendly and compatible, I decided I couldn't marry him, and he later married a very nice lady from Annapolis.

Perhaps the most serious of the attachments I formed was the one with Eugene Roberts. It lasted off and on for nearly six years. John and I first met Gene and his wife through the Who Dealt Bridge Club because they were invited to substitute occasionally. I think that our friendship began when I told him off! Not realizing that his wife had been the daughter of a Hungarian countess, who before her marriage had been a Vanderbilt, I declared,

"You people in Prince George's County are just so bound up in all your prestige that you never see anything much of the outside world!"

He was laughing all the while I was berating him, because he had lived all over Europe and the United States. After his wife died, he asked me for a date. Our first date was a candlelight tour of the old houses in Annapolis, and from then on I saw him several times a month. He took me over to Washington for dinner and dancing from time to time. Gene was a delightful person, but we had moved in very different circles, and his life was geared more toward Washington and Newport than toward Maryland. We broke up several times during the six years. His three children had been very devoted to their mother, and Gene finally decided to marry a French woman who had been a family friend.

Once more, I tried sheep at Obligation, and finally built up a herd of about 80 head. We had a problem finding someone who knew how to shear them, but we found a school teacher who did a good job. The wool paid for the upkeep of the sheep, and we had all the lamb we could eat ourselves and sold quite a few of the rest. John Phibbons was the cattle dealer who took them to market, unless someone local wanted to buy one or two. Eventually, the wild dogs discovered the sheep and began to come at dawn. Although we had the sheep in the barn, the dogs would get to one animal and tear it up so badly that it had to be destroyed. One of my patients was the Deputy Sheriff, and I asked him to come here to try to shoot the dogs early in the morning. The Animal Control people told me that they'd bring traps to catch the dogs. Of course, the dogs never came when we had traps, so I finally decided that we just had to sell the sheep.

We stopped raising tobacco at Obligation in the 1960's. At one time we were growing it on three farms and it was our only cash crop, but the price of tobacco hadn't increased for about twelve years, and the margins were getting smaller. It became more and more difficult to find a good tenant, and the entire enterprise became an unmanageable problem.

Most doctors didn't want to practice in the country because conditions were still comparatively primitive. There were two or three doctors who came with the idea of joining my practice at the Tea House. One was a periodic alcoholic, who would be fine for a while, but then would lapse, and tragically, he was killed in an automobile accident. Dr. Smith from Shady Side was here for a good many years. He was a very nice person, and we almost put together a consolidation, but he finally decided that he didn't want to consolidate because he'd had a large enough dose of country practice. Dr. Wirth was formerly a doctor for an insurance company in Washington. He moved to the country and opened his own office, but fortunately, he later decided to come in with me, and I was glad to have him. He was very well received by the patients, and he took my afternoon office hours after he arrived.

Dr. Wirth introduced me to peacocks. He maintained a collection of exotic birds at his home, and he gave me several cocks and three or four hens. At first we kept them in a pen to accustom them to the place so that when we released them they'd remain on the farm. The peacocks put on quite a show at the cocktail parties we held on the lawn. It was possible to hand feed them pieces of bread. Those peacocks were so happy at Obligation that they reproduced over the years to where we really had too many of them. There were 49 or 50, and the majority of them were cocks, which caused lots of fights resulting in lots of noise. They even became a hazard to people driving out on Rt. 2. There were peacocks everywhere. They roosted in the trees and on the seat of Chris' tractor when it rained. Bettie explained that the noise didn't bother her, but it did infuriate her when the peacocks visited their garden and stalked down the row of their tomato plants, puncturing each ripe tomato with their beaks. Then there was the problem of the deposits the peacocks left on their deck, making running about in bare feet risky business. Finally we had to cut back the size of our flock, and now we have only two cocks left.

# THIRTY-SEVEN

*She is the grandmother and has played a very important part
in their (the children's) growing up. I am the daughter-in-law,
and it made me rather nervous to move to Obligation. I wondered if she would come to the house to check on my housekeeping ... or if we were expected to invite her to dinner if we
were having friends in. But those things meant nothing to her.*
                                                    *Bettie Wilson*

I became a grandmother for the first time on June 4, 1968, when
a son, John, was born to Bettie and Chris. They were living in
Pennsylvania then, but her doctor was in Washington, so they
came down to Obligation for the last month of her pregnancy. As
I've mentioned before, babies frequently decide to be born at night,
and this baby was no exception. We all got out of bed in the middle of the night and prepared to get Bettie to the hospital. Chris
and I woke up hungry, so before we left for the hospital, we went
down to the kitchen to make some grits-and-kidney stew. Bettie
has never been able to tolerate that dish even in a non-pregnant
state, and under the circumstances I didn't blame her for becoming a little excited. While Chris drove us to the hospital, I sat in the
middle of the back seat spooning my portion of stew from an old
blue bowl.

My second grandchild, a girl, was born on August 14, 1970. She
was named Emily. She seems to have inherited some of her
father's personality. She has ridden horses all her life, loves the
country, and seemed to have a problem with regimentation when
she was a little girl. Emily was just two years old and John was
four when Bettie and Chris moved to Obligation to live.

Bettie's Aunt Ned lived in Upper Marlboro and was my good
friend. Frequently she came to Obligation to visit for the weekend,
and when she did, we would offer to babysit the children so that
Chris and Bettie could get away. One time when John and Emily
were very young, Bettie sat down and wrote several pages of
instructions for Ned and me. The instructions were very detailed
and provided information as to what we should be doing with or
for the children at each 15 minute interval. Needless to say, the
minute Bettie got out of the door, we threw the instructions in the
trash can. I didn't confess that to Bettie for several years.

Bettie began a custom of holding a Sunday night family dinner
to which I was invited. Bettie decided that it was a good opportunity for the children to learn "which fork to use" and for all of us

to catch up news of each others' activities. Each of the children had lessons and after-school sports activities of one kind or another, and the adults were also going in their own various directions. Discussions were quite lively, and I looked forward to the Sunday evening get-together.

Travel began to play a more important part in my life during these years. I suppose it was because I had a little more time and a little more money. For many years I'd had the care of the surviving members of the Wilson family, particularly Mrs. Wilson and her sisters. Occasionally, I could leave Mrs. Wilson with her daughter, Margaret, while I got away. Being able to leave my practice in capable hands was the biggest reason I felt able to take some time off.

I've been lucky to have visited a good many places around the world. My youngest brother, Julian, worked for the Commerce Department. His business was to set up trade shows in various parts of the world, and because of his overseas assignments and his hospitality, I've had many opportunities to travel abroad. In addition to visiting almost all of Europe, Teheran and Jerusalem, I took three trips to South America because Julian was stationed there. Usually, he could offer a chauffeur and automobile in addition to a room. Over the years, we visited Cuzco, Machu Pichu, and Buenos Aires.

Although Julian had visited nearly every major city in South America, there was one tiny corner of Columbia that he'd never seen. He decided this was a place he simply must visit, but he was recovering from major surgery and probably shouldn't have been thinking of such a strenuous expedition. Since I was visiting him at the time, I was invited to accompany him. Maybe he thought he would be in good hands with a doctor along. We started making plans, and learned that if we wanted to go from one point to another outside the city of Bogota, we'd have to fly back to Bogota before leaving to reach our next destination. The city is in a saucer surrounded by mountains even though it's at an altitude of 5,000 feet. Nearly always the mountains were hidden in fog or haze. Of course, the airplanes were rather primitive in those days ... old and rattly. Before our plane took off, the ground crew filled it with just enough gas to climb over the mountains. Once over the mountains, the plane landed on the jungle level to fill the gas tank before taking off again.

We flew for hours over the jungle to this place a thousand miles from Bogota. Although Julian had made reservations for us, when we arrived at the airport we were told that we must leave the following day. This was because the President of Columbia would be arriving and had commandeered all the rooms in the only hotel for his party. Julian had reserved rooms with private baths, but soon discovered that our accomodations were hardly luxurious. There was one sheet on my bed, and I decided to take it off and sleep on the obviously unclean mattress, wrapping the sheet around my head to ward off attacking squadrons of mosquitos. The next morning there was no hot water, so Julian ordered a thermos of hot lemonade to use for his shave, and we also used it for brushing our teeth. Then Julian used Scotch as his aftershave lotion.

We hired a small boat and set out in search of the headwaters of the Amazon River. Along the way, we found the source of water for the hotel, and we saw some lily pads as large as chairs. Later in the day, the weather began to deteriorate, the boat began to bounce in the waves, and we started back. We saw several logs in the water ... at least we hoped they were logs and not alligators.

The next morning, the hotel manager began to fuss about, urging us to get to the airport before the President's plane arrived. We hurried to the airport where we learned that our departure would be delayed because an incoming plane had skidded off the runway. Every able-bodied man, woman and child in the village was helping to push the plane off the runway so the President's plane could land. We waited and waited, becoming hungrier and hungrier because lunchtime had come and gone and we'd had very little breakfast. In desperation, I dug into the bottom of my handbag, and came up with some Metrecal packets. We mixed the Metrecal powder with Coca-Cola from the machine in the airport.

On another trip in the early 1970's, Stephanie Rich and I boarded a freighter in New York. There were only eleven passengers on the ship, and we wanted no one to know that I was a doctor. When the ship arrived in Panama, our cabin was filled with flowers which Ed Rich and Cory Cramer had sent to us. While the ship was locking through the Panama Canal, lunch was served on deck so that we passengers wouldn't miss any of the sights. One of the four ladies from New York was very blond, and she became painfully sunburned. Stephanie offered,

"You know, my friend is a vet. She may have something to help you."

I was able to give her some cortisone, because I always travel with a certain amount of supplies. We relaxed thoroughly on the freighter, and we were able to view interesting sea life from her decks as we traveled up the West Coast to San Francisco.

# THIRTY-EIGHT

*Tup was a wonderful foil for my mother ... He tempered her impatience. They were a wonderful couple together, and it was an extremely happy time for her.*

Christopher H. Wilson

The first time I met Albert Tupper Walker, I was 17 years old. Everyone called him Tup, and I was introduced to him at the home of a girl friend. From where I sat in the back seat of a car, I couldn't see exactly what he looked like. I made a bet with my friend that I wouldn't see him again, but when he called to ask me for a date I had to pay up a box of chocolates. We had a nice group of young people in the Beech Island neighborhood, and Tup and I went together to the dances and parties from the time I was 17 all through my medical school days.

He couldn't afford to go to college, so he had a hard time getting any kind of job, and that's why I never married him the first time. We didn't have any money between us, and for that reason my family was very much opposed to my going with him. I can't say I have many regrets, because to be honest, we would have had a difficult time financially. Times were very hard, and his family was even poorer than ours. There were six of them, and they seemed to be distantly connected to nearly everybody in the neighborhood. His father had never made a success of his life and had married a woman who was a little less than desirable. However, she turned out to be a fine, hard-working woman who kept the family going, and most of her family turned out very well.

When I left South Carolina for Maryland, our parting was very difficult. Tup came up to visit from time to time while I was at Hopkins because he got a free pass from the railroad. He was very anxious for me to marry him; but there remained family opposition, and I was just starting my practice, and additionally, I'd met John Wilson.

Tup had seen an advertisement in a magazine extolling the benefits of clip-on chains. He sent the chains to me in a big box, but did not include his name or return address. I thought that John had sent the chains because he knew I was frequently stuck on the terrible roads. When I thanked John, he smiled and accepted my gratitude without comment. It wasn't until much later that I learned that Tup had sent those chains.

Later on, Tup became interested in the timber business and worked for the Southern Railroad buying timber for cross ties. The railroad sent him to Guatemala frequently, and he developed a lot of sophistication, but I didn't know him during those years.

After I married John, Tup and I didn't see each other for at least thirty years. I guess that he was always in the back of my mind, because we had gone together for so long.

In the spring of 1972, I planned a large party at Kathwood for my niece prior to her wedding in Augusta. I invited all my old friends from Beech Island, including Tup and his wife who were once again living in the neighborhood. They were unable to come to the party because, unfortunately, his wife was ill with cancer; so I didn't see them at all during that visit. In January of 1973, I got a letter from my sister, who reported that Tup's wife had died. I wrote a note of condolence and received a prompt reply from Tup, who wrote, "I hope I'll see you before too long."

In May of that year, I went to South Carolina to visit Louise and Katharine. They invited Tup and some of my other friends from the neighborhood to Kathwood for cocktails. After that evening Tup invited me out to dinner every night, and we felt the old affection renew itself almost immediately. I was somewhat confused and uncertain, because, in the first place, I wasn't sure that I wanted to marry again, and there was the memory of family opposition 40 years before. In the second place, there were a lot of things to work out, such as the way our children might react ... his one son and my two ... and I had already been through one such unpleasant experience.

We corresponded after I returned from South Carolina, and he came up for the Fourth of July and then again in September. He was very anxious for me to marry him. Although my children were dubious at first, they began to accept him and eventually they became very fond of him. I think they realized it would take a load off their shoulders if somebody else took over the job of looking after me.

So it went along. When he flew up for the weekend, I met him over in Washington. He retired the first of January 1974 from his job in Augusta, and his son and daughter-in-law moved into his house in the country to live with him. He told me that he would be willing to come up to Maryland to live, but I still wasn't real sure. There was some question from a priest I consulted about whether we could be married until Tup had been baptized. Of course, Tup wasn't a Catholic, and he had never been baptized.

In May 1974, after another of his visits to Maryland, Tup returned to South Carolina, driving another widow and me along with him. Tup and I still hadn't made a decision, and on the way down to South Carolina, Tup teased me, saying, "I haven't quite decided which of you widows I am going to marry." My friend was very attractive, and I admit to feeling a little pang of jealousy. After Tup and I talked to a priest in South Carolina, the priest surprised us by saying,

"I'll marry you today, if you have the license."

We made the decision just about one week before we got married, and it was a very busy week. I found a pretty green chiffon dress, and one of my friends made me a corsage of magnolia buds to carry. My son, John, had had some foot surgery, and, since he was taking a medical leave he came to give me away. Tup's son was his best man, and my niece was my only attendant. We were married very quietly on a Thursday with our families as the only witnesses, and afterward my sisters gave us a reception at Kathwood.

On the way back to Maryland, we stayed for a quiet week on the Outer Banks before we returned to Obligation. Soon after we arrived home, we had a large reception for over 200 people under a big tent in the yard. Sam Pratt and his family catered the party for us, and, as he said later, "EVERYBODY was there!"

We settled in, and it worked out.

Tup's life had been so completely different from mine that I wasn't sure how he would fit in with my life in Maryland; but he did. In my life I'd had lots of people around, and social activities, and cocktail parties, but he had led a very quiet country life. For a while at the beginning he was somewhat lost because he didn't know anybody. He was a very relaxed person, very low key, and just perfectly happy to fiddle around here ... maybe read a little bit, and do errands. He was the cook when we didn't have a cook, and he declared he was a better cook than I was.

My best friends, Catrina Bowie and Stephanie Rich became very fond of him, and I never heard of anyone who didn't like him. We had lots of guests back and forth, and my friends accepted him very nicely. Tup was easygoing and ready to join in, but sometimes he protested,

"Oh, let's not go to that party. It's much pleasanter for us to sit down and have cocktails right here."

But after Tup got involved in the party, he had such a good time he frequently didn't want to come home.

Tup enjoyed young John and little Emily as much as I did, and we continued to do quite a bit of babysitting. As the children grew, Tup and I made a habit of attending John's baseball games and Emily's horse shows. Tup and John frequently listened to the ball games on Sundays, and Bettie continued her Sunday evening family dinners with Tup fitting right in. Little Emily had a problem with nursery school and kindergarten, having attended quite a few of each. Since Bettie worked at the Legislature part time, Tup was on call any day she was unable to leave in time to meet Emily after school. When Bettie called to ask Tup to pick up Emily, he'd ask, "Well, where is she this week?" Tup was fond of saying that fetching Emily from the various schools she attended was the way he learned his way around Anne Arundel County.

By the time I got home from the office at noon, Tup would think of some reason why we had to go grocery shopping. He had an obsession for a fresh doughnut every day for lunch, and fresh doughnuts were made daily at the Edgewater Giant. We'd go to pick up a few items at the Giant, always choosing a single doughnut. Finally, after several weeks of this practice, the girl behind the bakery counter asked,

"Do you mind telling me just who eats this one doughnut? Do you cut it in half?" I still laugh remembering that.

When I married Tup, I had been running the farm with the help of Mr. Sam Sillaman, a local farmer. It was Mr. Sillaman's custom to come up to the house every morning and sit down at the dining room table with us while we drank coffee and discussed the work to be done that day. Mr. Sillaman had a rather negative outlook about most things, and each morning when Tup looked out of the window to see him coming, he announced,

"Oh, my God, here comes the Cloud of Doom!"

Mr. Sillaman was with us at Obligation for a period of seven or eight years, managing the place and running the cattle herd. We also had chickens, and Mr. Sillaman took their eggs up to Parole to sell them. He was finally forced to curtail his activities because of poor health, and after Sam left, we had to make some changes.

Earlier, when I'd discovered that the crops didn't make enough money even to pay the taxes, John Phibbons and I went to a cattle auction and bought 20 Angus cows and a young Charolais bull. We developed a reasonably good herd of the Angus-Charolais cross. After Mr. Sillaman left, the care of the cattle became a real problem: the two Johns had to get up and feed them before going to work in the mornings, and it seemed that every Sunday the cows would push over a fence and get out of the pasture, intermingling with some of the neighbors' cattle. For a while our main activity on Sundays seemed to be chasing cattle. Tup was a little intimidated by the cattle, I think, and he was leery of going into the field with them. Bettie says her one firm memory of those years is running into the soybean field to round up cows. Tup finally sold the cattle herd and rented the farm to Bill McKee. Bill McKee did a good job of running the herd and raising hay, corn and soy beans.

Tup oversaw the construction of the summer house at Obligation. It is a place we loved to sit in good weather. Buddy Groves built it for us, but Tup accused him of using timbers that seemed too big and heavy for the purpose.

Buddy answered, "We are going to build this summer house strong so that if you have a heavy snow it won't cave in."

Tup grumbled, "We might as well add another story on top. It's strong enough!"

My medical practice continued actively, although the necessity of my being in constant attendance had been relieved by Dr. Wirth's joining my practice. I was delighted that Tup was willing to accompany me on visits to my patients in nursing homes, and I still made rounds at the hospital in addition to holding office hours.

Two changes of significance occurred during this period. The first was the appearance of the birth control pill. In spite of being a devout Catholic, I dispensed the pill because I believed then, and still believe, that there are families who need the means to limit the number of children they bring into the world. I remain adamantly opposed to abortion, whether legal or illegal. Although the rhythm method of birth control is very often inadequate, these days there are several methods which may be employed successfully to prevent conception. However, once conception has occurred, abortion, in my opinion, should not be considered an option unless the life of the mother is in jeopardy.

The second change rather saddened me. During all the years of my practice, most people had faith that the doctor was doing everything possible to help the patient. Naturally, not every case could be brought to a successful conclusion, and there was an occasional dissatisfied patient. However, the real possibility that I might be sued by a patient or his family had never entered my mind. I was advised that I could no longer be complacent about the good will of all of my patients, and, about ten years before I retired, I yielded to pressure and purchased malpractice insurance.

# THIRTY-NINE

Except for his business trips to Guatemala, Tup had never had much chance to travel, so we decided we'd go around the world. Julian was stationed in Hong Kong at the time and had a two bedroom apartment overlooking the city. Although we spoke to a travel agent about our plans, it was Julian who suggested most of our itinerary. He had visited more than one hundred countries and had lived in many of them, but he had never been to Katmandu, so we included a trip to Katmandu in our plans. Before we left Obligation, Julian advised us: "Put all your clothes and all your money out on the bed. Then pack half the clothes and take twice the money."

Louise, Catrina Bowie, Tup and I flew to Japan. We landed in Tokyo, and after a brief visit to Nagasaki, we went to Kyoto where we stayed in a Japanese inn. Although it was more expensive than a hotel, it was fascinating because it was so totally different. We had an entire suite, and Tup and I shared a room on a courtyard. The routes to the bathroom lay either across the courtyard or through the room shared by Catrina and Louise. The first time Tup tried the rocky courtyard route in his bare feet he decided from then on to go through the girls' room. We slept on futons, and the dining table in our suite was the height of a coffee table. A maid brought the supplies into our dining room and fixed our meals on a brazier. What delicious food! Everyone but me wanted American breakfasts, but I decided, "As long as I'm here, I want to see what the Japanese eat for breakfast." I was served bean curd, soup, salad, and a little raw fish for my breakfast ... and I ate it. We had a hot tub, and I was the only one who would try it. The procedure is first to take a bath, sitting on a low stool and washing, then using a hose to rinse off the soap. Only then do you get into the tub for a long hot soak. It was wonderfully relaxing, and I loved it.

From Japan, we went to Taiwan, where we had two or three days in the Grand Hotel. It was perfectly awful because the food was unbelieveably bad and getting into town was inconvenient. However, when we finally got to town to wander around a little bit, we saw a wonderful museum, built to house Chiang Kaishek's treasures, among them the most gorgeous porcelains. It is said that the exhibits are changed every six months because a cave in a mountain is filled with the treasures brought out of China.

We arrived in Hong Kong to visit Julian and his wife, Nikki, where Nikki had prepared good food for us, and we were able to get our laundry done and to catch up on other housekeeping chores. We stayed with them for a week, and while we were there we went downtown to visit the Republic of China stores. We nearly lost our minds, because we saw beautiful hand-embroidered linens and other lovely things at extremely reasonable prices. Fortunately, Julian was able to send some of our purchases back by the courier.

Julian and Nikki joined us for the remainder of our around-the-world trip, and from Hong Kong we went to Bangkok. Tup ordered a suit to be tailored at the hotel shop in Bangkok, and every time Tup walked past the shop, they would drag him in and start pinning the suit. It was a suit that fit him better than anything he ever had, though. We went to see the sacred city and the gorgeous buildings that were featured in the movie "The King and I," and we visited an exhibition city illustrating how people lived in the various areas of Thailand. We also took a canal trip. Afterward, we were in the hotel beauty shop getting our hair done when a most distraught woman came in wailing,

"Please, scrub my head good! I've been taking a shower for half an hour!"

She, too, had taken a canal trip. When her barge returned to the dock, all the passengers rushed to one side to get off. The barge turned over, throwing everyone into the canal! Fortunately, the water was only about eight or ten feet deep; but unfortunately, the sewage from the houses backing up to the canal went directly into the water.

In New Delhi we stayed at an old English hotel. It wasn't one of the finest ones, but it was comfortable, except that they were experiencing power outages. The hotel turned off their air conditioning in the middle of the day because the management had concluded that all the tourists ought to be out sightseeing. We saw gorgeous materials in the shops, and naturally we couldn't resist ordering some dresses made for Louise and me. Every evening a boy from the shop came on a bicycle to our hotel for a fitting. However, Louise inadvertently had left her camera in the shop, and not until we got on the bus for our tour of the Red Fort did she realize it was missing. She was sure she'd never see her camera again, but our bus driver happened to overhear her worrying about the missing camera and somehow communicated with the dress shop. While we were touring the Red Fort, where Gandhi had been cremated and interred, a young boy rode up on a bicycle and handed Louise her camera. We thought it unbelievable that a thing of such value was returned in spite of the terrible poverty in the country. I thought that New Delhi, and India in general, were pretty sad because of such wide-spread poverty, but also quite remarkable because of their history and culture.

We drove over to Agra to visit the Taj Mahal, and along the way, our driver had to dodge cattle lying in the middle of the road. If he had hit one of those animals, it would have meant a $1,500 fine and perhaps ten years in jail. It took three or four hours to drive the 100 miles!

I was prepared to be disappointed with the Taj Mahal because we had heard so much about it. People had told us that it was dirty. Well, it is absolutely immaculate, and we saw men cutting the grass with scissors and small hand sickles. The building itself is exquisite. Constructed of white marble, using no cement, the blocks were cut to fit together perfectly. Inlays of flowers made of malachite, lapis lazuli, and other semi-precious stones decorated the exterior. We were required to put cloth shoes over our street shoes both to protect the floors and to protect our feet. The floors were too hot to walk on in stockingfeet. The man who put the shoe coverings on our shoes was helping Catrina when our guide said, "Don't tip him until we come back." So the man promptly stopped what he was doing, and we had to remonstrate a great deal with him before he would finish the job. He got his revenge, though, because he gave Catrina a shoe cover which flapped as she walked. We called her "Big Foot" for the rest of the day.

We had scheduled more touring, but it was 10:30 in the morning and already 110 degrees, so we asked our driver to take us somewhere to get a cold Coke. He drove us into a little town and stopped at a corner "joint." We entered and noticed several men and women relaxing under the ceiling fan around small tables. The minute we walked in, the women jumped up and whipped aside a curtain, disclosing a sizeable jewelry store at the back of the room. Catrina, Louise and I chose to sit at the counter the better to investigate the jewelry, while Nikki and Julian sat under the fan drinking nice cold Cokes. From their table, they laughed at us, warning,

"You will be buying nothing more than glass."

Rubies are my birthstone, and I really wanted a ring, so, thinking I'd never have another chance to get one, I had purchased a ring with tiny rubies in it for about $80 while we were in Bangkok.

"I see you like rubies," said one of the men to me. He must have recognized my downfall, and he went back to his wall safe and removed a tray of jewelry. He selected a ring with three antique pigeon blood rubies in it, assuring me that it had belonged to a maharaja's estate. He explained that he and his father had broken up some of the most elaborate jewelry, using the stones in new designs. He claimed that he was willing to write a note certifying the stones to be antiques. Of course, I was a little dubious, because he had no one to recommend him; but we started talking, and I learned that his father had been to Johns Hopkins to have surgery, and he was acquainted with some of the doctors there. He assured me,

"We have a store in Philadelphia, and if you don't like this ring when you get home, or if you have it appraised and find it isn't worth what you are paying for it, we will take it back."

So I thought I'd take a chance: I liked it, and I bought it. Catrina bought about $5,000 worth of jewelry, a beautiful emerald bracelet, and Louise bought a ring or two. When we got home, I took my ring to a jewelry store on Main Street in Annapolis, and the jeweler exclaimed, "These are very rare stones!" He sent the ring up to New York, where it was appraised for double the price I'd paid for it. I've frequently thought about that taxi driver who took us for a Coke at a place which "just happened" to be a jewelry store.

At last, we went to Katmandu. Mr. and Mrs. Owens, my neighbors, had been to Katmandu a year or so before, and they told us about hiring a small bus to cross a mountain to see a particular ceremony. The ride over the mountain was gorgeous, but the ceremony turned out to be a yearly sacrifice. It took place near a stream partway down a valley where the people would bring small animals, goats mostly, all decorated around their necks with flowers and bells. Then the priest cut the animals' throats, allowing the blood to run over a wall as a sacrifice. Afterward, the people were allowed to dress these animals and take them home for food. Although Tup and I thought the little valley very pretty, we didn't think too much of the ceremony, so we just walked back up the steps to the bus.

We took an all-day trip in a small minibus to see the Anapura range. We stayed at Fishtail Lodge, a fairly new building built in a semicircular shape where each room had a wonderful view framed by very large windows. The big attraction was to wake up at precisely the right moment to watch the rising sun paint the snow pink on top of the mountains. Even though the hotel desk had promised to alert us, we woke up from the time it first cracked dawn. Although we dressed and went out, we really could have stayed in bed to watch the sunrise through our picture windows.

On our return trip over the mountain we saw the most beautiful irrigation system I've ever seen. It was all natural and must have been in place for many centuries. Rocks had been placed to support the small terraces, and there were fruit trees and rice and vegetables growing at an altitude of 12,000 feet. There were no pipes or pumps, but the water came as natural drainage from the melting snow. I sat in the front of the bus, and chatted a bit with the driver.

I asked him, "What happens around here when somebody is

seriously hurt?"

He pointed to weeds growing along the roadside, and said, "They stew those up and feed it to you. That's marijuana."

We stopped for lunch at a large flat rock on the side of the road, and before we could eat, we were surrounded by several children who were caring for herds of cattle. They looked so hungry that we offered to give them some of our lunch. The driver said, "Let me divide the food myself." He knew that if he simply handed the food to them, the children would fight over it and only the strongest would get anything. After lunch, when we got near the 12,000 foot divide, the bus began to overheat. We had carried some thermos bottles of cold water with us, so we got out and poured one thermosful into the radiator. We thought we might have to push the bus back to Katmandu, but we coasted down the other side of the mountain.

Leaving India, we flew to Frankfurt, Germany, where we had a six hour layover. Instead of permitting us to go through Customs during the long hours in Frankfurt, we had to wait until we arrived in Hamburg, where we got off with all our luggage, went through Customs, got back on the plane, and continued to Helsinki. We arrived in Helsinki at 10:00 at night after a 23 hour trip! One of Nikki's friends met us with two cars and took us to a small hotel on the outskirts of the city. We had a wonderful time because Nikki has two or three sisters and brothers living there. The cleanliness of Finland, the food, and the immaculate dining rooms were quite a contrast to what we had left behind in India.

I thought we'd never get ourselves together the next morning, but somehow we did and spent the day sightseeing. We toured the countryside on every kind of transportation you can imagine. We went on the train, and we went on the bus, and we went in private cars into the little villages. The countryside was beautiful, and every speck of it cultivated and cared for. It was wonderfully cool after India. It was the end of May, and fortunately, there were heavy dark shades at our windows or we might not have been able to sleep, for the sun was still in the sky. We saw a man sitting on a park bench reading his newspaper at 2:00 in the morning.

While we were in Finland, we took the opportunity to join a Finnish tour to Leningrad. When we got to the Russian border, two soldiers went down the aisle of the bus collecting our passports in a basket and removing all the baggage. Everyone was unloaded from our bus to go through Customs, and Nikki did the translating. We were asked to open our wallets to show how much Russian money we had. We were delayed for an hour and a half while the border guards took a dog through the bus, and they even got out ladders and climbed on the top. We never did find out if they were searching for something specific.

Leningrad, or St. Petersburg, is a fascinating city, even though it was almost destroyed during the War. The downtown office buildings have been rebuilt so that the exteriors appear exactly as they did before the Revolution, but we were told that the interiors of the buildings were cut up into cell-like rooms. The Winter Palace had not been touched, and still held marvelous treasures. I have seen a great many museums all over the world, but I think this is the most fascinating one I've ever seen. Every room is full of wonderful art, and there are tiny Battersea boxes, and jewelry, and furniture that belonged to the royal family. Julian found an English guidebook, and he became our tour director ... not that he knew anything more about it than the rest of us. Russian visitors clumped around on the museum's beautiful parquet floors in their rough boots. One small Russian woman sat near the door to an exhibit room, keeping an eye on the visitors. One person started to pick up a Battersea box to take a better look, and she warned, "No touch! No touch!" It was probably the only English she knew, but it was effective because the box was put down like a hot potato.

Peterhof, a palace outside of town, was built by Peter the Great. We were unable to tour the Palace because it had been completely destroyed during the War and was undergoing restoration. We were allowed to tour the restored gardens. There was water everywhere and bridges over small streams, and fountains, beautiful fountains. One particular spot in the gardens resulted in quite a shock to the unwary person who stepped on it. A hidden button activated a fountain, thoroughly spraying the visitor.

Our tour bus picked us up and took us to a tourist hotel which accomodated 5,000 people. Although the building was quite new, all the chairs in the lobby had broken seats and the leather coverings were nearly all gone. Visitors to this hotel were completely regimented. We were ordered to be at our breakfast at 8:00 a.m., and we had exactly 15 minutes to eat it and then had to leave the table so that the next group of tourists could be seated.

We flew home from Helsinki feeling very lucky that we had been able to see so much of the world.

# FORTY

To celebrate my fifty years of practice in southern Anne Arundel County, my office staff and my family planned a party in my honor. The party was meant to be a surprise to me, and for a while it was; but somehow these things develop a life of their own, and I learned of the plans ahead of time. I was greatly touched and gratified to learn that my patients, both black and white, came together and worked on plans for the party. The church hall at Our Lady of Sorrows was decorated and all the food prepared by my patients. Someone began requesting contributions to a special fund, and with the money collected they bought a beautiful gold bracelet which was presented to me as a gift. I was overwhelmed by the great number of my friends and my patients who attended, some from quite a distance. The Gotts came down from Pittsburgh, and my sisters came from South Carolina. My friend, Aris Allen, was the Master of Ceremonies, and introduced Virginia Clagett, a long-time friend and member of the County Council, who gave a little speech. Fortunately, there weren't very many speeches and those were blessedly short. During the party, many people came up to remind me, "You brought me into this world," and I finally had to warn Sam Pratt,

"You are getting to be a gray-haired old man! Don't you go around telling everybody I brought you into the world. It makes us both seem old."

I was amused to consider that perhaps people were trying to tell me something, such as, "You've been practicing long enough, and it's time for you to retire!" However, I didn't take the bait, if bait it was, because I didn't retire for three more years. In truth, I had come to believe that it might be time for my retirement, but I didn't want to leave Dr. Wirth alone with the patient load. After Dr. Jones agreed to join him at the Tea House, it began to look as though my retirement might be possible. I thought that I might have to leave town for a while before my patients became accustomed to it. We had to educate some of them a little, but for the most part, they were really very cooperative. I had set the date as September first, 1982, and that morning I simply didn't go into the office. I may have celebrated by sleeping a little later that day, even though I've never been a late sleeper. Tup, of course, was delighted with my retirement, and we never seemed to be at a loss for something to occupy our time.

Tup and I took a trip to Egypt where Julian and Nikki were then living. We took the boat up the Nile to Aswan to see the temple at

Abu Simbal. Other passengers on the boat included a couple from New Zealand. They ate at our table, and we noticed that they seemed amused by us. Finally, we asked them why. They answered that in New Zealand, a male sheep is known as a tup.

In an attempt to preserve some green space so that development would not consume all remaining undeveloped land, the county began the Conservation Easement Program. One real incentive for entering this program was to achieve a reduction in property taxes because each time our property was reassessed, the taxes went up. I talked it over with the boys and with Tup, and we all agreed that we wanted Obligation to remain a farm. I had given Bettie and Chris five acres on which to build their house, and I had given John the Red House and five acres. In about 1980, I gave them some additional acreage so that they each owned outright about 15 acres surrounding their houses. In determining how to proceed with the Conservation Easement Program, Jack Rouse was a big help to us, but even so, it took almost three years to complete the paperwork.

Although the county was anxious to make it happen, I think it was such a new program that they didn't really know what they were doing, and it seemed they put in every possible roadblock. We had to arrange for three appraisals of the place to get some idea of what it might be worth if the property were to be developed, as contrasted to its worth as a farm. The county's intention was to pay the difference to the property owner. After three years, the county finally arrived at a figure, but it was many thousands of dollars less than the last appraisal.

"Take it or leave it," said the county officials, "and you must decide right away."

Tup decided, "I think you ought to go ahead with it," so we grudgingly accepted the offer. However, Bettie's father, a very smart man who does my taxes, determined that I could call the difference a gift to the county, so I got my revenge! This agreement means that Obligation will remain a farm not subject to development for the foreseeable future.

Once or twice a year Tup and I drove down to South Carolina to see family and friends. We both enjoyed these visits, and the trip was easy with two of us driving. However, he had begun to complain that he thought his glasses needed to be changed, and we went to see an opthomologist. The doctor told me that Tup was in the first stages of a deterioration of the retina in one eye. He really put it on the line, telling us,

"Even though one eye is still pretty good, he is probably going to lose all the central vision in both eyes."

One day when we were driving home from South Carolina, we

were stopped at a traffic light just after crossing the Potomac River Bridge.

Tup said, "I can't see what color that light is."

The next day we returned to the opthomologist's office and learned that Tup had had a hemorrhage in the back of his good eye. From that time on, he had only peripheral vision but no central vision in either eye.

After seeing the doctors in Annapolis, we decided to go to Johns Hopkins to learn if there might be anything that could be done for Tup's condition. They encouraged us, "It just might be that we can use a laser and restore at least some of your sight." But after spending an entire day at Wilmer Clinic while doctors injected dye into Tup's eyes, performed tests, and studied the whole problem of his sight, the doctors reported, "We are very sorry. The blood vessels are dead and there is nothing we can do. However, your condition will not get any worse, and you will never be totally blind." That news was some consolation, of sorts.

He rarely complained, but every now and then he would become irritated if he was unable to do something he wanted to do. We received the Washington Post, the Baltimore Sun, and the Capital. He had been in the habit of spending most of his mornings reading the papers, and more than anything he missed being able to read. He eventually located an all-news radio station which he listened to during the day. When I'd read some of the newpapers to him, he'd say, "Good Lord, I heard all about that yesterday on the radio!" He couldn't read his papers, and he couldn't drive a car, which were the two things he missed most of all; but he had his radio. He was able to watch football games on TV if he sat to the side of the set, and he was still able to do some of the cooking.

Always willing to run errands and to drive me when I was tired, Tup was frustrated with this condition, but he took it in his stride most of the time. Fortunately, he never became completely blind.

# FORTY-ONE

Beginning about Christmastime in 1987, Tup wasn't feeling very well. He hadn't been eating, and he had lost some weight. He didn't complain of pain, so it didn't seem to be anything to worry about. However, one morning about the middle of February 1988, he said,

"I feel terrible! I can't drink my coffee this morning, and I don't want anything to eat."

We went promptly up to the hospital and found Dr. Steve Hiltabidle. Dr. Hiltabidle put his hand on Tup's abdomen and said,

"We've got a blockage. I'm going to admit him and see if we can get this obstruction cleared up with the usual things. If we can't, I may have to go to surgery."

He advised me to go on home because the procedure was going to take a while. I'd hardly entered the door when he called to tell me that he had sent Tup to have some x-rays, "But," he said, "I'm going to have to do a colostomy right away."

I returned to the hospital immediately. Tup's surgery went off well, and Steve waited for about a week after Tup left the hospital so some healing could begin. When we went to see Steve a week later he reported,

"I think we can remove the tumor in the bowel and put things back together." We were very optimistic after hearing that; but when they again took Tup into surgery and opened him up, they found that the growth had gone into his kidney and the abdominal wall.

Tup didn't come up from the Recovery Room for so long that I began to worry, and I finally found the anesthesiologist. She told me that Tup had had a reaction to veratrin, and they'd had to put him on a respirator. Veratrin is something the Indians had used for their poison arrows, but modern medicine uses it as a muscle relaxant. When they took him to the Recovery Room and began to give him oxygen, Tup was unable to breathe on his own. They were working on him while Steve came up and told me the bad news.

With great compassion, Steve told me, "I'm very sorry, but there just isn't anything we can do for him."

I said, "I want to go down to see him."

The anesthesiologist said, "I don't think you do."

"I'm going anyhow," I said.

I found Tup to be in a panic because he was awake and couldn't breathe. I was able to calm him, telling him,

"I'm here, and everything will just take a little time."

The following morning Steve and I went together to tell Tup the results of his surgery. It's a terrible thing to have to do. Lord knows, I've had to do it often enough, but when it hits close to home, it is devastating. It was Steve who told Tup,

"My friend, I'm truly sorry, but you have only about six months to live."

In a few days, Tup was back at home, and for a time he really came back quite well. The colostomy was working, and no one knew better than we how to take care of it. In May, we went down to Kathwood for two weeks, and we had a nice time, but all the while Tup was losing weight.

Upon our return to Obligation, we placed his bed in the den downstairs, but Tup wasn't confined to bed until just two weeks before he died. By then, his weight was down to 110 pounds. He had insisted on getting up and walking to the bathroom, and Tup walked with help to the bathroom, even on the day he died: July 23, 1988.

It was his wish to be cremated. We held a memorial service at Our Lady of Sorrows, and then we took his ashes back to South Carolina to be buried in our community cemetery at Beech Island.

We'd had a very happy fourteen years together ... longer than we thought, really, because he was 70 and I was 69 when we married, but I think it was almost harder losing a husband the second time. When John died the boys needed me, and I had my practice, and I was very busy at the hospital. After Tup's death, especially after being entirely occupied with his care, suddenly there was very little for me to do. I had to start all over, and I'm not quite sure how I did it. One simply does. Of course, all the family helped by keeping me busy, but to start living alone again is very difficult. Now it seems quite natural, and sometimes there is so much going on that I really don't have time to do all I'd like.

The family made my eighty-fifth birthday in 1989 very special. My brother, Chris who lives in Savannah, arranged with the State of South Carolina to hold a joint birthday party for me and my eighty-year old sister Katharine at Redcliffe. Busses took everyone from town out to the plantation. At least two hundred people attended, and we filled the old house with family and friends. It was a wonderful party!

In 1990 by way of another diversion, Bettie suggested a trip to Great Britain. Since I had been three times or more to England and Ireland, Bettie offered to let me decide where we'd visit. Bettie, Chris, and my sister Mary, and I had a marvelous trip through Wales and Scotland. We drove through the Lake Country and stayed in an old castle in Wales. Scotland was chilly, and the wind nearly blew us off the parapets of Edinburgh Castle. When we got to Heathrow Airport, Bettie ordered a wheelchair for "her feeble old mother-in-law, who can't stand on her feet very long." Then they decided that since Mary also had gray hair, she, too, could play the invalid. They piled all the luggage in our laps and we sailed right through Customs, by-passing the long lines and the red tape. When we arrived at our gate, Mary and I were "parked" near the Duty Free Shop, and Mary was so eager to see what was available that she got out of her wheelchair; but I was afraid to get out of mine because I was supposed to be an invalid.

# FORTY-TWO

*I now pay rent to live at Obligation. Officially I am a tenant because I own neither the house nor the farm.*
                                                                    *Emily H. Wilson*

Back in the 1960's when our neighbor Mrs. Zantzinger died, all of us were appalled to learn that the largest benefactor of her estate was Uncle Sam. We took a look at what the situation might be at Obligation, and we became uncomfortably aware that we might have a similar circumstance. From time to time we discussed our options, but we never were able to get the thing settled. Finally, I was determined to come to some resolution and heeded the advice of Ron Holden, an estate planner. Early in 1986 I deeded Obligation to Tup and we formed two trusts, with John as trustee for the trust containing the house and ten acres, and Chris as trustee for the trust containing the farm. Tup would have had the place for the remainder of his life if I had predeceased him, but he died first. Unfortunately, when John and Chris inherited, they had to pay very high inheritance taxes because it happened to be at the very top of the real estate market.

Although the prime reason for this bit of estate planning was to remove from my estate its major assets, another result was to free Tup and me from the daily problems of upkeep of the farm. It was a difficult transition for all of us, and after the many years of managing and caring for the farm, I found it impossible not to notice things that needed to be done. Tup threatened to fit me with blinders so that I couldn't see left or right when we drove out of the road.

Tup's death precipitated quite a few changes. It was obvious that we had to do something about the operation of the farm because we couldn't continue shoveling money into it just for the privilege of living here. Bill McKee, after several years of farming the place, decided that he needed more money than he was making, and he had to leave. Afterward we had help from a series of neighboring farmers. The permanent maintenance of the farm began to suffer, and Chris found fault with nearly everything, probably because he thought he could do a better job. Although he had not yet retired, Chris gave the tenants notice, and when their lease terms were over, the farm reverted to him.

Chris realized that he had to do something in a hurry to make the farm begin to pay its way. He rented 35 acres to Ricky Davis, who planted soy beans and corn, and who has ever since continued to do a very good job of farming. Chris bought seven or eight steers, which he kept on his own property. The first year he made about $200. The second year he bought more steers, but it was a disaster, because he lost $2000, and he complained that owning the farm was worse than having a child in college. He was very discouraged and felt trapped by his situation.

Chris and Bettie had fixed up a small barn on the property so that little Emily would have a place to stable her riding pony. There were four stalls in the barn, and the three unused stalls were rented to help defray Emily's show expenses. These three rented stalls were managed by Emily. Then Chris built a board fence enclosure to use as a paddock. The first year, they had the cattle and the stable operation running at the same time, and of the two, they decided it was much easier dealing with horses than with cattle. Gradually, Chris began to believe that one way out of his dilemma was to begin a horse operation.

He had a terrible time getting the pastures back into shape. They were grown up with cockleburrs and wild artichokes, and for three years, Chris did nothing but mowing and spraying and reseeding. I had a small problem with Chris when he told me that he needed to clear out trees along the fence lines. I hated to see the trees come down, even though I understood the necessity for it.

There were two tobacco barns on the farm which were not being used, but taxes were being paid on them, nevertheless. At the same time as he cleared pastures, Chris started his new venture in the old tobacco barn by building stalls and a hay loft with lumber cut on the farm. People who needed a place for their horses began to find the farm, and the business grew. Lumber to refurbish the second barn was also cut on the farm, and when it was finished, Chris and Bettie engaged Linda Stanier to manage it. Chris was so encouraged that he bulldozed a riding ring and hung lights for night riding. Eventually, the horse operation was turned over to Linda to manage, and she has been quite successful.

As Linda's business burgeoned, periods of inclement weather made it impossible to schedule lessons sufficient to satisfy all the people who wanted them. Chris felt that from the standpoint of remaining competitive, it was necessary to construct an indoor riding facility. The new riding arena was built from scratch. He had help from a farmer/barn builder from Calvert County, who, along with his two sons and two laborers, constructed the indoor arena. It turned out surprisingly well and was paid for by adding more stalls to handle more horses. We have about 40 horses boarding at Obligation, with a lot of activity from riding lessons and horse training and trail rides. New housing developments are underway not far from the farm, and we expect many people to take advantage of the open space available here. We have miles and miles of riding trails, and riders can also ride cross-country through neighboring properties.

One by-product of our horse operation is the great amount of manure generated by our four-footed boarders. We have found a way to market it rather than trucking it away. We produce excellent compost!

Obligation, the farm, has gone through many changes since I bought it as an apparently worthless property so many years ago, from tobacco farm to cattle farm to horse operation. The horse operation seems to be the key which will permit the place to remain a self-sustaining farm. The future here looks pretty good for all of us.

Obligation, the house, also has had a recent change or two. We had some floors sanded and we replastered and repainted in the den, making a terrible mess. I have every intention of remaining here, so we contacted three or four contractors to determine whether an elevator could be installed in the stairs. We didn't want the stairs to be changed in any way, and we wanted to be sure that any elevator could be removed without lasting damage. The contractors complained about the narrow stairway, mentioning that no two treads are exactly the same width and no two risers are exactly the same height. I asked them just what they expected in a house nearly 350 years old! Finally, we found a contractor who has managed to satisfy our requirements, and we have had the stairway elevator installed. By way of keeping fit, I have prescribed for myself one trip each day up and down the steps under my own steam. Of course, I fell recently and bumped all the way down the steps.

Thanksgiving 1995 brought together at least 16 members of the family at Julian and Nikki's new house in Fernandina Beach, Florida. Before we started out for Florida, I decided that I ought to get a new car to drive and chose a new Cadillac with all the latest bells and whistles. The saleswoman took my driver's license to complete the forms, and as she returned it to me, she exclaimed, "I'm afraid there is some mistake here. This license says you were born in 1904."

"No mistake, at all. It's quite correct." I answered.

Do you think she wondered why a 91-year old woman was buying a new car?

Fortunately, I remain able to drive my car, to work in my gardens, to entertain visitors, and I enjoy parties and people as much as ever.

I'm going to keep going until I get old.